BRAIN
WAVE
VIBRATION

BRAIN WAVE

VIBRATION

Ilchi Lee

Getting Back into the Rhythm of
a Happy, Healthy Life

**BEST
LIFE**

BEST LIFE

BEST Life Media
6560 Highway 179, Ste. 114
Sedona, AZ 86351
www.bestlifemedia.com
1-877-504-1106

Second paperback edition: November 2009
Library of Congress Control Number: 2009939001

ISBN-13: 978-1-935127-36-9
ISBN-10: 1-935127-36-5

If you are unable to order this book from your local bookseller, you may order through www.bestlifemedia.com or www.amazon.com.

Printed on 30% post-consumer recycled paper.

For the many people working to create
health, happiness, and peace in the world.

A human being is a part of the whole,
called by us universe, a part limited in
time and space. He experiences himself,
his thoughts, and feelings as something
separated from the rest——a kind of optical
delusion of his consciousness. This delusion
is a kind of prison for us, restricting us
to our personal desires and to affection
for a few persons nearest to us. Our task
must be to free ourselves from this prison
by widening our circle of compassion to
embrace all living creatures and the whole
of nature in its beauty.

—Albert Einstein

FOREWORD

ILCHI LEE'S PREMISE IS simple but compelling. We are all human; what we have in common is more profound than what divides us; we must find the wisdom and the will to rise above our parochial geographic, religious, and cultural differences and to embrace the human universals. To promote these values and to graft them onto the collective consciousness of humankind, Ilchi Lee has undertaken a multipronged effort that is nothing short of astounding in its diversity, energy, and global reach.

Advancing our understanding of the brain, brain health, and public education about the brain has been among Ilchi Lee's foremost interests and the focus of his activities. He is the founding president of the University of Brain Education, president of the Korea Institute of Brain Science, and president of the International Brain Education Association (IBREA). The educational outreach of these organizations includes online lecture courses; conferences on various aspects of brain development, and mental and emotional health; annual Brain Olympiads; and a magazine titled *Brain World*. These organizations are remarkable for consistently involving in their activities a diverse group of educators, clinicians, and scientists, including myself. It is precisely because of its global outreach that I find my role as a scientific adviser to IBREA so gratifying and ripe with opportunities for making a difference worldwide.

Ilchi Lee's work has been honored with numerous awards and has been warmly received in important forums around the world. Many of his educational initiatives are conducted in association with the United Nations, which offers a unique platform for making a global impact.

As an individual, Ilchi Lee is a multifaceted personality. He is a teacher, a philosopher, a musician, a martial arts practitioner, and a talented organizer of global initiatives. He is also a prolific, insightful, and original author with several influential books to his credit. *Brain Wave Vibration* stands out as capturing and summarizing the essence of his philosophy and training methodology. In our times of stress, strife, and uncertainty it conveys with great force a message of optimism, hope, and equanimity. It is written with simplicity, clarity, and depth.

Brain Wave Vibration consists of two parts and several appendixes. The first part, titled Principle, synthesizes some of the state-of-the-art insights and findings of neuroscience, Eastern philosophical and spiritual traditions, and mental and physical health cultures. The book's narrative is particularly impressive in its seamless interweaving of diverse approaches and cultural traditions. The strength of the Western intellectual tradition is in its rigorous analytic nature. It tends to take things apart and examine the components in isolation from one another, but it has been historically less successful in putting things back together, resulting in a somewhat compartmentalized and disjointed view of the world.

By contrast, the Eastern intellectual tradition tends to emphasize unity and fluidity, yet sometimes lacks rigorous definitions and analytic approaches. These differences have been historically a source of societal disconnect stymieing mutual understanding and cross-cultural integration. Ilchi Lee is able to take the best from each tradition and create an impressive synthesis integrating the two. He is also able to integrate into a coherent narrative elements of diverse domains too often treated as separate: neuroscience, cultural anthropology, the arts, and philosophy and ethics, to name a few. As a result, his book conveys a powerful message of cultural unity and universalism through a unique bridge between brain science and practical applications. The combination of scientific (including neuroscientific) and experiential foundations constitutes the approach espoused in the book and makes it attractive to the reader.

In the second part, titled Practice, Ilchi Lee describes a range of ingenious exercises designed to enhance physical, cognitive, and emotional well-being. The exercises are described in considerable detail. They are quite diverse, and together they amount to a comprehensive physical workout. But the underlying premise is that these exercises also contribute to mental, emotional, and spiritual well-being, and enhance the functions of the brain.

Some of the impetus behind the design of the exercises came

from Ilchi Lee's own experience of overcoming the effects of an accident and his—as it turned out, very successful—efforts to regain his own health. The ability to look adversity straight in the eye and turn it into an opportunity is what defines a person's caliber of character. It speaks to the strength of character and personality, and this strength of Ilchi Lee's personality and character comes through in much of his work and accomplishments.

Ilchi Lee describes how the Brain Wave Vibration exercise began with a single person, recovering from the effects of a stroke, who joined him in a park in Korea. Today the following is vast; it extends across countries and continents. Some of the success stories resulting from practicing Ilchi Lee's exercise routines are recounted in the appendix "Stories of Healing and Hope." The array of individuals who have benefited from the exercises is impressive. They come from various countries, walks of life, age groups, and occupations. It is clear from these accounts that the benefits bestowed by the exercises are multifaceted, improving many aspects of one's physical, emotional, and spiritual health, as well as one's ability to overcome the effects of stress and to communicate with other people.

Brain Wave Vibration is rich in themes, thoughts, and potential impact, and can be read and enjoyed on many levels by a diverse readership. It will be of particular interest to those seeking physical, emotional, and spiritual self-improvement. It will also be of considerable interest to those in search of interesting facts about the workings of the brain and the mind; about the complex interactions between the brain and the rest of the body; about the fusion of our physical and spiritual beings, and the fusion of diverse cultural traditions and philosophies; and about the nature of happiness. It will be of great interest and value to those in a state of physical or emotional distress seeking to regain a sense of well-being. And it will also be of interest and value to those already enjoying a sense of well-being but seeking to enhance it even further and attain a higher level of fulfillment and self-realization.

In a world preoccupied with material gains and now in turmoil brought on by material excesses, recklessness, frivolity, and greed, the ability to put things in perspective, to have a deeper purpose in life, to rise above the turmoil, to be at peace with oneself, and to find a spiritual anchor is a precious gift. Ilchi Lee's wise and insightful book provides an invaluable guide toward accomplishing all these goals.

Elkhonon Goldberg, Ph.D.

Elkhonon Goldberg, Ph.D., *is a psychologist, scientist, author, and educator. He is a professor of neurology at New York University School of Medicine and director of the East-West Science and Education Foundation. He is dedicated to the study of the brain's complex cognitive processes, to clinical work, and to teaching. His books, including* The Executive Brain: Frontal Lobes and the Civilized Mind, *have been translated into several languages, and he lectures worldwide.*

CONTENTS

Part 1: Principle

Part 2: Practice

ACKNOWLEDGMENTS

RARELY IS A LONG JOURNEY success-ful when taken alone, and such is the case with this book. This book is culmination of the work of many bright minds and passionate hearts, and I would like to extend my sincere gratitude to all who have contributed to its creation, as well as to all of those who have supported its highly successful distribution after its publication. In the preparation of the second edition, I am especially indebted to all those who offered their personal expertise to help improve the book's content. In particular, I appreciate the scientific guidance provided by psychologist Dr. Matthew Kelly, neurologist Dr. Elkhonon Goldberg, and physician Dr. Sung Lee. Great gratitude must also be extended to the entire BEST Life Media team for their hard work and professionalism. Finally, I would like to thank all of the many thousand individual practitioners who, through their dedication and diligence to their own healing, have helped establish the effectiveness of Brain Wave Vibration, especially those willing to share their personal journey on these pages.

The Case for Brain Wave Vibration

THIS BOOK IS ABOUT a training technique so easy to understand that you really don't need a book about it. The technique is Brain Wave Vibration, a healing and self-development method that anyone can learn in two minutes. This method is so simple, in fact, that complete instructions could easily fit on a single piece of paper.

So why, you may ask, would I bother with this book? Why not just pass out photocopies of that single sheet of paper? Or maybe post a video on YouTube or spread it through Internet discussion boards? Well, because I want you to understand just how deeply transforming this method can be, and I want to share my passion for it with you. I have seen many people achieve remarkable results through this method. I think it can change people's lives for the better, and I am hoping you will discover the same.

This book, as well as the training method that is its subject matter, is based on one very simple, but unusual premise: your brain is your key to health. Just as you train your body, it is time to train your brain. Your brain creates your life and controls your health. Thus, it is time for you to take charge of your brain through Brain Wave Vibration.

I am not only arguing for the method itself. Rather, I wish to convey that you have tremendous untapped power within you—power to heal, to create, and to love—that is waiting just below the surface of your being. Brain Wave Vibration exists solely to help you uncover that natural ability.

The Birth of Brain Wave Vibration

Actually, I have been teaching Brain Wave Vibration for years. Previously, I called it *Jin-dong,* which literally means "vibration exercise" in Korean. The purpose of this training was to open the energy system of the body for improved health. In those days, the focus was on the flow of energy through the body in the more conventional sense of traditional Asian medicine. Through the years, however, I have come to realize the role of the brain in this process. Thus, the name for this training is now *Noe-pa-jin-dong,* the word *noe-pa* meaning "brain wave." The brain orchestrates our bodily functions, and it is through the brain that we make the choices that determine the quality of our life experience. As my understanding has increased, I have come to see that the brain is the key to mental and physical health.

My initial interest was to create health through the enhanced flow of energy in the body. I began simply by teaching stretching exercises in a park, drawing upon my training in martial arts and Asian medicine. At first, only one person came—a man who had suffered a stroke. I worked with him to stretch his body and to open the meridians that carry energy through his body. Over time, he gained more and more movement, attaining a remarkable degree of recovery.

As the years went by, I began to realize the important role of the brain in the healing process. I had some indication of this connection years earlier when, in a moment of great epiphany, I felt a sudden change take place in my own brain. It was like my head was about to explode, and then suddenly everything seemed clear and an unshakable sense of peace and oneness came over me. Yoga, tai chi, and other forms of exercise could produce good results, but the effects were always temporary if more fundamental changes did not take place in the mind and, more specifically, in the brain. Thus, I developed the Brain Education System Training method, which brings various mind–body training methods together in one cohesive form (see page 256).

As I gathered a larger number of students, I worked on developing more training methods, hoping to find the simplest, most effective means of returning people to physical, mental, and spiritual health. The results included Dahn Yoga (energy training), DahnMuDo (a gentle, healing form of martial art), Jung Choong Energy Breathing, and many other mind–body development exercises and techniques.

Many of these methods are very effective, but they all require a certain amount of guidance to understand and practice. I was still seeking the simplest mode of healing, one that could be instantly understood and practiced by anyone. Brain

Wave Vibration, a refined variation on the old *jin dong* technique, turned out to be just what the doctor ordered.

A Fortunate Fall

A lot of great things in this world have been discovered by accident. Alexander Fleming, for example, discovered penicillin when he accidentally left a Petri dish uncovered. A few years ago, I took a bad fall from a horse and seriously injured my spine. The process of nursing my body back to health taught me a lot about the importance of vibration and movement in the process of healing.

My accident happened back in 2006 when I was out riding my horse Su in Sedona, Arizona. As we were slowly trotting along the dusty red rock trail, something suddenly spooked Su. He reared up and galloped away at full speed. I lost hold of the reins as he ran wildly across the dessert landscape. When I reached down to grab them, Su bucked me off. I flew through the air and landed flat on my back, which cracked loudly as I hit the ground.

After the fall, I could barely move my spine. Each movement felt like a hot spike was inserted into the vertebrae. The doctors told me not to move, to just quietly rest in bed. This did not sit well with me because I knew that the energy could not move properly in my body if I were just to lie there completely motionless. So I decided to make subtle shaking movements with my spine and eventually with the rest of my body. This kept my energy moving, and my recovery was far faster than anyone thought possible.

Soon, much sooner than anyone thought possible, I was up and walking again. As I took my first feeble steps, I remained acutely aware of the effects of vibration in my body. What before had seemed like a horrible accident now seemed like a great blessing; the painful process of healing seemed to have heightened my ability to perceive and understand the nature of vibration in my body.

My experience inspired me to take a second look at *jin dong*, the old vibration training technique I had used on occasion before. Previously it had been a simple accessory training, but now I began to apply it more rigorously in the training sessions that I lead. Through the process of working with hundreds of people toward the relief of a variety of mental and physical conditions, I revised the practice into the method you will see described in detail in the "Practice" (pages 163–197) part of this book. I was and continue to be astounded by the elegant simplicity and amazing efficiency of this method. I have seen it change people's lives in dramatic ways, as is evidenced by the "Stories of Healing and Hope" on pages 203–241. Because it is so easy to learn, I think everyone should be encouraged to use as a simple self-healing technique.

The Benefits of Brain Wave Vibration

Beyond the principles and theories that underlie Brain Wave Vibration, the most critical aspect is the concrete benefit you receive through actual practice. If you practice sincerely and with an open mind, I think you will be surprised how soon you will begin to experience benefits.

The best way to understand the benefits of Brain Wave Vibration is to actually do it. In the back of this book you will find detailed instructions and suggestions that will help you make the most of the practice. Nevertheless, you can actually start right now, right here while you are sitting here reading this book.

All you have to do is put this book down and gently shake your head back and forth. Close your eyes and concentrate on the movement of your head going back and forth. Just focus on the natural rhythm for one or two minutes—back and forth, back and forth. Go ahead—put the book down. I'll see you in a couple of minutes.

So how was that? Even though you did this simple form of the technique for only two minutes, I am willing to bet that you felt some difference. Perhaps you felt a bit more relaxed, maybe the tension began to release from your shoulders, or maybe the world looked a little bit brighter when you opened your eyes.

If you were able to feel something in two minutes or less, imagine what you might experience with prolonged, consistent practice. In the second section of this book (pages 163–197), you will learn how to go deeply into the vibration and to alter its form to suit your specific needs. While this motion is simple and easy to follow, in reality it can help unleash a cascade of healing effects: increased blood flow, loosened spinal nerves, reduction of brain wave frequency, and stimulation of the vestibular system. Everyone's experience with Brain Wave Vibration is unique, but here are some of the major benefits you can expect to receive:

• **Physical Benefits:** Brain Wave Vibration will move your entire body, promoting cardiovascular fitness, improved circulation, and better strength and flexibility. It helps reduce the stress response in the body, inducing a state of deep relaxation. The vestibular system will be stimulated by the movement of the body, helping to modify and coordinate information received from the body for better equilibrium. Finally, it will stimulate the body's innate healing ability as you open up the body's energy system.

• **Mental Benefits:** Just as your body will relax, so will your mind. As you learn to clear your mind of extraneous thoughts, you will also learn to shake off burdensome emotional memories. Your mind will become clearer, and you will be able to access your full creative potential. As you empty your mind of old, debilitating thought patterns, you find new ways of approaching problems and limitations. As you send positive messages to yourself, you will also gain a new sense of confidence and self-determination.

• **Spiritual Benefits:** As you go deeper into the practice, you will become aware of the energy field that binds us all together, while also solidifying your personal sense of life purpose. Compassion, loving-kindness, and gratitude will flow naturally from your heart. Your life will become a reflection of your internal sense of integrity. Through Brain Wave Vibration, you can glimpse the sense of expansion and oneness spoken of by the world's great spiritual sages.

Putting the Brakes on Stress

Stress is perhaps the number one reason that people need Brain Wave Vibration. Many people are caught in an almost constant state of stress and it is having a detrimental effect on mental, physical, and spiritual health. I would even go so far as to say all the problems in your life relate, in one way or another, to the experience of stress in your life. If you can learn to manage your stress, you have learned to manage your brain; if you have learned to manage your brain, you have learned to manage your life. Brain Wave Vibration is a simple and effective way to manage your brain for increased health, happiness, and peace.

The stress response, in and of itself, is not a bad thing. It is merely a survival response that can help us think and move more quickly in a dangerous situation. When you perceive danger, your brain sends signals to the autonomic nervous system, which then triggers the sympathetic or "fight or flight" response. The heart rate increases, blood pressure rises, and muscles tighten.

This is all very helpful in a life-or-death situation, and it can be helpful for the body and brain when experienced in small doses. But unfortunately, perhaps due to our busy, competitive lifestyles, many of us are stuck in a nearly constant state of low-level stress, which leads to great wear and tear on the body. Brain Wave Vibration is one way to begin to manage the stress response and to break the mental patterns that keep us caught in unhealthy brain wave states.

It has been well documented that stress is related to a number of chronic diseases—heart disease, hypertension, diabetes, irritable bowel syndrome, fibromyalgia, to name only a few. But I think physical health is only one of the victims of the stress habit. I believe that gaining control of stress is essential to mental and spiritual health, as well as physical health.

An Evolving Awareness

Over the years, I have worked with hundreds of thousands of people all around the world, most of whom have made great strides toward greater health and well-being. I began with a single student in a park more than thirty years ago, and as the word of its effectiveness spread, more and more people came to experience it for themselves. Today it is a movement that includes 3,000 instructors in 1,000 centers in North America, Europe, and Asia. Well over one million people have experienced the benefits of Brain Education. While Brain Education may include a variety of techniques, I believe that Brain Wave Vibration is the easiest and quickest method to increase an individual's well-being.

My Brain Education method has grown out of the Eastern mind–body development traditions. Yet, you will notice as you read this book that many scientific studies are mentioned. However, I am not a neuroscientist, a doctor, a psychologist, or a scientist. I first understood the principles that form the foundation of Brain Wave Vibration experientially, rather than intellectually, through my studies of traditional Korean energy training and martial arts. Yet, I retain a very deep respect and admiration for those who do study these things scientifically, and I remain confident that one day there will be a meeting of the minds between these Eastern and Western ways of understanding the world.

Brain Wave Vibration and the Brain Education method has not, as yet, been studied completely by the scientific community. Two studies, one conducted at Cornell University and the other at Osaka University, have shown the positive effects of Brain Education on psychological health and the perception of well-being. Also, a Japanese hormone researcher, Arita Hideo of Japan's Toho University, has shown that Brain Wave Vibration increases levels of serotonin, a hormone associated with relaxation and a sense of peace and contentment. However, interest is increasing, and some investigation has begun. You can read about the latest inquiries in the second appendix, page 242–147.

The Source of Miracles

Brain Wave Vibration training is ultimately about freedom—freeing your body and brain to work as they were always meant to work. Life is supposed to be free and organic, but we often suppress our brain's natural abilities through the stress and emotions we habitually feel. Every living creature possesses a natural healing ability, which is essentially the ability to bring one's body back into equilibrium. The fact that over 85 percent of modern people suffer from stress-related illnesses suggests that we are not fully utilizing this innate ability to heal.

In a way, this training helps you integrate your neocortex with your brain stem. If you are under continual stress, it is likely that your brain stem cannot create equilibrium in your body. Your neocortex, which is the thinking part of your brain, is continually sending messages to your brain stem that keep you in a fight-or-flight state. For example, your thinking mind may continually generate messages like "You are not keeping up with the competition" or "You are not being a responsible parent." Hearing the alarm generated by your brain, your sympathetic nervous system puts your body into the fight-or-flight state, which increases your heart rate, brings tension to your muscles, and generates a host of other bodily effects.

The parasympathetic nervous system is also there, waiting to return the body to the rest-and-digest state, but if you cannot learn to quiet the messages of alarm from the neocortex, you will be left in an almost constant state of stress. Eventually, the stress response creates great wear and tear on the body, and many stress-related problems come about precisely because the brain stem is never permitted to create balance in the body.

So how do you get around this vicious cycle? Just let the brain stem do its work. If your neocortex is constantly creating negative messages about your life and the world in general, your brain stem will continue to generate a negative response for your body. Brain Wave Vibration training can help you calm your thinking mind and clear this negative information so that you can consciously choose positive, healthy information.

If you come to this book looking for healing from stress or other physical difficulties, this book has something to offer you. If you come plagued with negative emotions, like anger or depression, this book has something to offer you. If you simply come looking for ways of creating more meaning in your life, this book has something to offer you.

I believe that Brain Wave Vibration can help you create miracles in your life. You were probably not taught as a child to realize what a marvelous creature you really are, because your parents were not taught this important truth either. If you learn anything from this book, I hope you come to understand your inherent power, the power that is contained within your brain.

The technique does nothing to you, apart from helping you ignite your own body's healing ability. If you can uncover that, I think you can uncover a miracle. Because really, creating a miracle is just a matter of coming back to who you already are.

Reclaiming Our Wisdom

If all of these benefits seem too good to be true, I understand. It may seem like magical thinking to believe that something so simple could produce such good results. But really, the healing is happening within you. Your brain already instinctively knows what your body need for health and happiness. The method only helps you activate it.

Thus, in order to convince you of this method, I must first convince you to believe in yourself. You may have a decent amount of self-confidence and a relatively high level of self-esteem, at least in the usual psychological sense. But if you are like most people, you don't fully realize the power you possess.

At some point in humanity's ancient past, it seems that we stopped believing in our own inherent power. Many of the world's mythologies speak of a time during which all human-ity lived in harmony with itself and the Earth, such as Adam and Eve in the Garden of Eden. Disharmony came when people collectively agreed that power comes from somewhere outside themselves. Like Adam and Eve reaching for the fruit, humanity collectively began to grasp for control of the Earth and each other. They invented gods and kings and fought over which one should be given supremacy. All the power they needed already existed within them, but unfortunately they had forgotten this.

This turning outward has ultimately been a blessing in its own right, a fortunate fall of sorts, helping us gain rational understanding of ourselves and the world. Many advances in science and medicine were made possible through the ability to perceive difference, to categorize, and to analyze. But now the time has come once again to acknowledge the intuitive side of ourselves, this time with an expanded sense of awareness and purpose. The rational mind has served us well, but there is potential in our brains far beyond surface-level rationality.

I believe that all people possess amazing ability within themselves, thanks to the marvelous features of the human brain. In fact, everything I speak of in this book is already inside you, waiting to be uncovered. I am here only to offer guidance as you rediscover this vast storehouse of potential within yourself.

Better Brain, Better Life

Brain Wave Vibration is a tool for honing your ability to create your life with intention. Most likely, I do not have to convince you that your thoughts are powerful and that positive thoughts are the key to making a better life. But you also know that it can be difficult to put these ideas into consistent practice in your life. You may have tried to follow the advice given by teachers, only to be disappointed as the same old problems reappeared and a deep sense of dissatisfaction returned to you.

I would like to suggest that if you have had difficulty making your reality follow the wishes of your mind, it is because you have not taken the time to change the tool with which you can change your reality. In other words, you have not taken steps to train your brain.

On the surface, it is easy to convince yourself that your thinking is positive, but in reality you may have many layers of negative thought that can undermine even the most sincere effort for positive change. Brain Wave Vibration offers a way to break through the layers of self-negating thought patterns so you can shake them off and begin again. For this purpose, we will look directly at the bodily organ that produces thought—the brain—and we will attempt to tap into its full ability through a remarkably simple and effective technique.

If your thinking and habits are not synchronized with your higher intentions, it is probably because detrimental behaviors and thought patterns have been wired into the structure of your brain through years of repetition. Fortunately, neuroscience shows that we have an amazing ability to change the connections within our brains. Brain Wave Vibration is a way to clean the slate, so you can begin using your brain as you really intend.

Most of us have been conditioned to think that the answers to life's problems are complex. We look to complicated, obscure theories and scientific learning that require experts with years of study to interpret and apply. Also, we tend to think that problems arise from somewhere outside ourselves. Thus, we look outside ourselves for the answers. I am hopeful this book will help you rediscover that everything you need for health, happiness, and peace is already inside you.

The Big Leap Forward

Unfortunately, some people today have already accepted their limitations as permanent. They look at their lives and say, "This is my best. This is good enough." They just follow blindly and emptily through a succession of routines and social obligations. They look at the troubles of the world and say, "There is nothing I can do." These are the sleepwalkers of humanity. Unless they can wake up and realize their real potential, they are essentially already dead. The denial of one's own infinite power is one of the greatest sources of misery in the world, and many people are tragically caught in the trap of believing in truncated, shrunken versions of themselves.

At times, it may indeed appear to you as though the world is spiraling downward. And in fact, it is not certain that we will ultimately make the right choices to ensure our collective survival. However, there is a tremendous amount of hope to be had. People are beginning to use their brains to process information in ways that heal, rather than hinder, their fellow inhabitants of planet Earth. Humanity, I believe, is awakening.

They say that necessity is the mother of invention. Well, you might also say that necessity is the mother of evolving consciousness. The human race, and the Earth on which we rely, is up against a wall. At this point, it is a matter of evolve or die. I believe that we are presently on the verge of a great leap forward in human consciousness.

I know you are not one of the sleepwalkers. You are waking up, and you can see the vibrant beauty of the world around you, a world with which you are one, a world that you can also help create. But you must not sit in bed wondering what to do with your day. Get up and start creating your world. Your life is like one quickly passing day. You must get up and make the most of everything it offers.

PART I

Principle

CHAPTER 1

Life Is Vibration

People say that what we're all seeking is a meaning for life...
I think that what we're really seeking is an experience of
being alive, so that our life experiences on the purely physical
plane will have resonance within our innermost being and reality,
so that we can actually feel the rapture of being alive.

—Joseph Campbell, mythologist

YOU ARE A BEING DESIGNED to perceive vibration. All of your senses are made to collect different kinds of information from the world around you through vibration. When you look at something, your eyes are receiving and processing the waves of light as they appear in the form of shape and color. When you hear, your ears funnel in the vibrations of sound, which your brain translates into meaningful interpretations of reality. When certain oscillations and combinations of sound are especially pleasing, you call it music; when the sound of words is moving, you call it poetry. When you touch something, you perceive the dance of molecules beneath your fingertips—some moving quick and hot, others slow and cold. When you run your fingers over an object, vibrations inform the peripheral nerves just below the surface of the skin, helping you make judgments about shape, size, and texture. Even when you smell and taste, the experience depends on the vibratory interplay of molecules interacting with your own molecular makeup.

What we often do not realize, however, is that we are vibration-producing creatures as well. Of course we can sing and talk with our voices, which are ways of making sound vibrations. But there is another kind of vibration that cannot be so easily perceived with the five senses. It is an especially powerful form of vibration called thought. While we may not often perceive thought as being real in the same way that an object is real, it is in fact the most real and powerful thing in the universe.

Every achievement of humankind—from prehistoric paintings on cave walls to rockets blasting into outer space—all began with a thought conceived in someone's brain. We communicate these thoughts also by means of vibration—through the words we speak, the ways we touch, and the actions we take. When our thoughts find accord with those of others, amazing things happen and even entire planets can be transformed—sometimes for the better, sometimes for the worse.

There is one key player in all this vibratory communication. It is what is responsible for receiving, producing, and interpreting the vibrations that shape the quality and content of our lives. It is the human brain.

Brain Connections

All of your five senses depend on messages in the form of vibrations reaching your brain. But you have one more sense of which you may be less aware. You have felt this sense if you have ever had your mood affected by someone else. Perhaps you were in a persistently glum mood, and suddenly a cheerful person lifted you out of your cloud. Or maybe the opposite happened, and someone's internal anger contributed to your own growing sense of irritation.

This phenomenon stems from the brain's apparent tendency to resonate in accordance with other brains. You know already that your brain produces vibrations called brain waves. This cannot be directly observed, but I believe that these brain waves literally interact with other brains as we interact with people. Thus, we have an effect on others, and they have an effect on us before we have even said a word. And of course, our eventual words and actions in the world will also follow the dictates of these waves.

A scientific study conducted in 2003 offers interesting confirmation of the connection between brains. In that study, EEG readings were recorded simultaneously from two human subjects. The individuals were in two separate acoustically and electromagnetically shielded rooms. One subject was given stimulation that would produce predictable effects on the EEG readout. The other was given no stimulation. Amazingly, both

EEG readings were affected to some degree by the stimulation, suggesting that the two subjects were influencing each other's brains, despite being physically separated (Wachermann).

I think you can begin to see why I emphasize the health of human brain waves. These waves do so much to determine the quality of our lives, and we could do so much to change our lives if we could only learn to control our brain waves. Even long before I developed such a keen interest in brain waves, I began to notice how my mind could subconsciously influence those around me.

Young children, perhaps because their brains are so open to influence, are an especially accurate mirror of their parents' brain waves. I remember when my two boys were very young how quickly they would respond to my state of mind. Their moods often seemed to depend on my mood and that of their mother. Back in those days, I worked as a clinician in a local medical laboratory. For the most part, it was not a bad job, and I usually came home happy. My family and I would sit down contentedly and enjoy a meal together.

But occasionally, things did not go so well for me at the lab. Perhaps I was inundated with far too much work, or a client was not entirely cooperative. Whatever the reason, I would come home with my head full of negative thoughts and emotions, as though there were a dark rain cloud above my head. That cloud would grow and grow, like a developing thunderstorm, until every member of my household was under the dark shadow. The kids sulked, their mother nagged, and I grumped. It was as though we were all feeding on each other's negativity until it was practically unbearable.

I'm sure that you, too, have experienced situations like these, when a person's mind-set becomes contagious. I now believe that this is the direct effect of one person's brain waves upon another's. Fortunately, it can happen in the opposite way, too, as people spread positive thoughts to one another. But unfortunately, far too many people find their relationships destroyed by the influence of habitually unhealthy thought patterns.

Some people, perhaps through natural personality traits or through the example of very positive parents or role models, have already learned to control their thoughts, at least to a certain degree. They can instantly redirect their minds in a positive direction, no matter how dreadful the situation. But most of us do not possess such a high degree of control, and thus we need some tool, like Brain Wave Vibration, to help us shake off the burdens of life.

In retrospect, I wish I had had a method like this when I was a young parent. Imagine if I had taken a few moments during the day to feel the rhythms of my body, like you did earlier in this book. With each frustration of the day, I could have stopped for a few moments to return to a neutral place rather than building up a stockpile of stress and tension to carry home at night.

I am sure it is not difficult to see how the quality of your brain waves affects the quality of your life. If you can get hold of your brain waves, you can also overcome many obstacles in your life. I am here to teach you that you have more control over your brain waves than you might think, and Brain Wave Vibration is a simple way to exercise that control.

The Language of Life

If your brain waves can have such a dramatic effect on other people, imagine what kind of effect your brain has on your body! Your brain is in constant communication with your body's various organs and processes. Although we do not precisely know the role of brain waves in this process, it stands to reason that healthy brain waves can help produce a healthy body.

In fact, medical science is increasingly willing to acknowledge the connection between mind and body. It is clear that our attitudes and emotions can affect our overall health. But how are our body and mind connected?

I believe that all the body's systems are connected through a system of energy channels. Cultures all over the world have sensed that such an element exists and have given this energy many names. The Pacific Islanders call it *mana*; Australian Aborigines call it *joja*; Indian Hindus call it *prana*. Native Americans have many different names for it: *maxpe* (Crow), *waken* (Dakota), *manitou* (Algonquin), to name a few. In Asian cultures, it is known as *chi*, *qi*, or *ki*.

You can feel this energy simply by quieting your mind. Close your eyes for a few seconds. Breathe deeply and just feel the essence of your being, without any thought or judgment. Can you feel the energy's vibrations running over the surface of your skin? Can you feel it emanating from the interior of your being? Maybe you feel heat or a slight tingling sensation somewhere on your body. This is your vibration—the vibration of life, the vibration of the universe.

Science, tending to reject that which cannot be directly observed, usually dismisses the notion of life energy as superstitious and irrational. In the past, however, many scientists sought proof of what they called *élan vital*, an invisible life force that animates living creatures. Unable to find such proof, most scientists have tended to prefer a more mechanistic understanding of life, and they reject this concept.

However, they do know that one measurable form of energy does play a role in the body—bioelectricity. Bioelectricity is the language used by the brain to communicate with all the organs of the body, telling them when to spring into action, when to speed up, and when to slow down. Signals are sent down through the nervous system via nerve fibers, which signal a myriad of biological processes, from muscle movement to organ functions.

Furthermore, we know concretely that the brain transmits its own special brand of energy, called brain waves, which are associated with various states of consciousness. Interestingly, it is now the absence of these waves, rather than the cessation of the heartbeat, that indicates clinical death.

Although we can't see or feel brain waves in the literal sense, they can be detected with the right equipment. Scientists use a high-tech machine called an electroencephalograph to measure the frequency of brain waves. As this equipment has become more sensitive, it has become clear that brain waves are quite complex. One can generally place them into five basic categories based on relative frequency: delta, theta, alpha, beta, and gamma. This chart represents the five brain wave states and the mental states associated with each:

TYPES OF BRAIN WAVES

DELTA	2–3.9 Hz	Deep sleep, unconsciousness
THETA	4–7.9 Hz	Deep meditation, sleep
ALPHA	8–12.9 Hz	Relaxed wakefulness
BETA	13–30 Hz	Everyday activity
GAMMA	30+ Hz	Intense mental activity

In reality your brain is like an orchestra playing an elaborate symphony, each "instrument" playing its own special part in harmony with the rest. The harmonies and tones change in accordance with our thoughts, moods. and emotions. When we call upon our brains to execute a certain task, it is like a conductor cueing a new musical phrase to begin. Brain waves are just one indication of the kind of music your brain is playing at a particular time.

As you can see in the chart, as the intensity of mental activity increases, brain wave frequency also generally increases. Natural health proponents agree that we are spending far too much time in the higher-frequency beta and gamma waves, and too little time in the lower-frequency waves. The higher-frequency waves are associated with stress states, which in turn are associated with many mental and physical disorders.

This is not to say, of course, that some brain waves are good and that others are bad. We need all these different states of consciousness at different times in our lives. It would not be a good idea to be in the deeply relaxed theta state while trying to navigate a car through a rainstorm. In that kind of situation, higher-frequency brain waves help people think and respond more quickly. Many of us, however, have developed the habit of staying stuck in stress-inducing, high-frequency brain wave states, which over time can take a serious toll on our health.

Fortunately, people can learn to control their brain wave states for improved mental and physical health. Eugene Peniston and Paul Kulkosky have shown that biofeedback, a method by which subjects are trained to control various biological functions, can be used to help people with alcoholism overcome their addiction. These two researchers developed a specific treatment plan for alcoholics that allowed patients to train their own brain waves through EEG biofeedback. Peniston and Kulkosky theorized that consuming alcohol is a way that people self-medicate for stress and depression. Through thirty biofeedback training sessions, a group of ten alcoholic men learned to increase lower-frequency alpha and theta brain waves, which are associated with a peaceful, meditative state of mind, and to control higher-frequency beta waves. In other words, they developed the skills needed to cope with and change unhealthy brain wave states. The training resulted in significantly less depression and fewer cravings for alcohol among the subjects when compared to a control group of ten men given a traditional alcoholism intervention program. And in the thirty-six month follow-up study, only two of the ten men relapsed, compared to eight of ten in the control group.

A friend of mine, in fact, is a researcher in the area of biofeedback, specializing in measuring brain activity through EEG machines. He was very skeptical about the claimed benefits of Brain Wave Vibration, like many other scientists might be. But he gave it a try anyway because he was suffering from a number of ailments and wanted to find a quick stress-relief exercise that could fit his schedule. After a few weeks of practice, his focus improved, his headaches disappeared, and his shoulder pain subsided. He is now thoroughly convinced that brain physiology can be influenced through movement of the body.

It is also clear that even the kinds of thoughts we have can greatly affect our physical health. The effect of the mind on the body was demonstrated by scientists more than a hundred years ago. In one experiment, scientists showed fake flowers to highly allergic people. Almost invariably, the subjects, not knowing that the flowers were fake, had allergic reactions when seeing the flowers (Sapolsky).

How the brain generates thought remains one of the major mysteries of neuroscience. However, we do know that certain kinds of perceptual states create very specific bio electrical rhythms as the brain's neurons communicate with one another (Hutcheon). It is not known how these rhythms may affect the other bioelectrical messages in the body, but it is likely that there is some effect. For centuries physicians have noted the placebo effect, in which a patient's beliefs about a given medicine may create as much healing as the medicine itself.

Matthew Kelly, an acquaintance of mine who is a specialist in psychophysiology, believes that what is typically called the placebo effect is in reality the psychophysiological intelligence of the body reestablishing the body's natural balance. He believes that the body's amazing ability to regulate itself, although influenced by environmental factors such as diet, fitness, and mental attitude, is built right into the system. In fact, Kelly goes as far as to state that it is the only thing that ever heals us. When a doctor treats us, he is really just assisting our body's inherent ability to heal.

Consider the story of a video arcade owner that I once knew. He had a quick temper and found himself constantly irritated with the kids in his arcade. This anger spilled over into every part of his life. His body became very tense, and eventually blisters appeared all over his skin. Worried about his health, he came to a Dahn Yoga center and began practicing Brain Wave Vibration along with the regular class, which includes stretching, breathing, and energy development training.

After only ten sessions, the blisters disappeared and his mind-set totally changed. Not only did he get along better with his young patrons, but he suddenly felt motivated to teach kids Brain Education techniques in a special after-school program. This man learned to reverse his negative brain waves, and the effect on him and those around him was almost miraculous.

For the sake of your own health and happiness, as well as that of so many others around you, please pay attention to the quality of your thoughts. People spend many hours honing the shapes of their bodies through weight lifting, aerobic exercise, and other athletic endeavors. Shouldn't people pay equal attention to the fitness of their brains? Behind almost every illness and relationship problem lies some habit related to unhealthy brain waves. Healthier brain waves translate into healthier emotional states, which in turn create stronger bodies and happier lives.

Coming Full Circle

The shamans of the past, and perhaps those existing in the present, were essentially brain wave doctors. They did not have the scientific understanding of brain waves that we possess, but it is clear that their healing systems were designed to stimulate healing power from within the ailing individual. Often this involved vigorously shaking the body or dancing frenetically until a deep state of trance was achieved.

Michael Winkelman, a neuroscientist at Arizona State University who investigates shamanistic practices, concludes that these healing practices work by integrating older (i.e., the brain stem) and younger (i.e., the prefrontal cortex) parts of the brain. He says, "Shamanistic healing practices achieve this integration by physically stimulating systematic brain wave–discharge patterns." This integration allows "unconscious or preconscious primary information processing functions and outputs to be integrated into the operations of the frontal cortex." In other words, the rational, conscious part of the brain is able to harmonize with the brain stem, the part of the brain dictating the subconscious operations of the body.

More recently, vibration has become popular as a way to develop bone density and muscle strength in older people. By simply standing on an oscillating platform, subjects who were otherwise quite limited in mobility were able to achieve improvements in bone density and muscle strength similar to those achieved through vigorous daily physical exercise (Olaf). In another study, thirty seniors were given strength training combined with whole-body vibration administered through an oscillating platform. In comparison with a control group of thirty seniors given strength training alone, those given vibration training gained much greater improvement in knee and ankle strength and mobility. The researchers theorize that vibration increased the bioelectrical impulses in muscle tissue, thereby increasing the rate at which the muscle can gain strength and flexibility (Rees).

Vibration also appears to improve communication between body and brain. In a study at Boston University, groups of fifteen young and twelve elderly subjects were given vibrating insoles for their shoes. The participants were asked to walk as the researchers measured the amount of postural sway present in their gait, both before and after the insertion of the insoles. They found that all groups reduced the amount of sway, which suggests improved balance ability. The improvements were most pronounced in the older group, whose average age was seventy-three. The researchers theorize that the vibrations improved the transmission of nervous system signals from the feet to the brain, thus overcoming some of the loss of balance usually associated with aging (Priplata).

It is not too great a leap to suppose that brain–body communication could be improved throughout your body if vibrations were applied to the entire body, as in Brain Wave Vibration. It seems that we are returning to an understanding that our ancestors understood instinctively.

I first experienced the power of vibration through my own physical healing falling from a horse, which I described in the introduction. As I taught myself to walk again, I discovered that even tiny adjustments in body position could make a big difference in how vibrations flowed through my body. As I adjusted my gait and posture for maximum healing benefit, I corrected bad habits I had developed long before the accident happened. As it turned out, I had been walking like an old man for quite a while without even realizing it. I began to observe how people walk, and I noticed that, for the most part, younger people walk with a spring in their step that fully uses the body's vibratory energy. Older people, on the other hand, tend to take a walking posture that stagnates the natural vibrations of walking, ultimately compromising their own energetic vitality.

My own healing process lead to the creation of a method called Jang-saeng Walking (see page 196), which uses proper alignment of the body and stimulation of the *yong-chun* energy point on the ball of the foot. Numerous studies have already confirmed the health benefits of walking, and I believe that part of the healing results from the vibrations inherent to the process of walking. As each footstep comes in contact with the Earth, vibrations run through our bodies, opening us up to healing energy. The human body is designed for walking, and it is unfortunate that modern life offers fewer opportunities for this natural healing method. Walking, like the vibrations it produces, is part of the natural wisdom of the human body and brain, and perhaps the most natural form of Brain Wave Vibration.

Returning to the Long-Lost Wisdom

Bradford Keeney has traveled the world seeking understanding of primitive healing customs. His conclusion, like mine, is that healing can be found through vibration, what he refers to as "shaking medicine."

Through his work, Keeney has noticed commonality among the world's many ancient native healing practices. All of them rely on the achievement of a deeply relaxed state, which is associated with low-frequency brain waves. This state can also be developed through the practice of meditation, which usually is achieved through complete stillness of mind and body. But in the most primitive cultures, this same state of relaxation is reached through ecstatic movement, such as dancing and shaking, rather than through physical stillness.

Keeney hypothesizes that this state of deep relaxation is what allows the subject to experience the healing effects. The thinking mind is quieted, allowing the healing powers of the brain stem to take effect. I contend that a similar state of deep relaxation is achieved through Brain Wave Vibration.

There is an essential difference between the modern psychiatric and medical approaches to a problem and the shamanic approach to a problem. The former tries to solve the problem through rational understanding, while the latter accepts the ineffable nature of human existence. Modern psychology has developed many useful ways of dissecting and defining a problem. Shamanic traditions, on the other hand, accept that a vast, incomprehensible universe exists within each person, and that total understanding is an impossible goal. Thus, a psychologist might prescribe external treatments to the problem, such as psychotherapeutic drugs or group therapy meetings to help the individual discuss and dissect the details of an issue. A shamanic healer instead guides the individual to go deeply within himself or herself to uncover the underlying spiritual roots of the problem. As Keeney describes it, primitive healing practices help move the person "into the mystery of life," rather than attempting to obliterate the unknown through rational understanding of things.

I am told that the word *heal* in English is derived from a word meaning "to make whole." I believe that Brain Wave Vibration offers a path to wholeness for practitioners. It is fine to seek a rational understanding of what troubles you, but ultimately you will need to go beyond the rational to really get in touch with the vastness of your being. Within that vastness, you will find the eternal wisdom and healing that has always been yours from the beginning of time.

Getting Connected

If you lack health in any form, whether mentally, spiritually, or physically, or if you are simply interested in maintaining the health you have, then you must seek the wholeness that gives rise to health. And this, I believe, means keeping connected with yourself, with other beings, and with the universe.

First, you must reconnect to your body. Allow your brain to connect properly to all the functions of your body, a process that is often disrupted by the stresses of life. Visualize the amazing web of living communication that exists within you—your brain sending its messages to your body and your body sending messages back to your brain. Consciously send a message of loving gratitude from your brain to all the cells of your body—they, in turn, will thank you for it.

Next, start to observe your own brain waves and their effects on others. When you speak of connecting to others, realize the literal truth of this, and you will soon be able to act according to your highest ideals and aspirations.

As you begin Brain Wave Vibration, it is important to do so with specific, positive intent. Without this, the action is only shaking, which might provide some temporary relaxation and escape, but it will not be permanent. Instead, as you shake, let go of everything and go to a place of oneness, the quiet center at the core of your being. It is from this place that you can begin to re-create yourself and to create the life you truly want to live.

CHAPTER 2

Hearing the Rhythm of Life

*Music, because of its specific and far-reaching metaphorical
powers, can name the unnameable and communicate the unknowable.*

—Leonard Bernstein, composer

IF YOU REALLY WANT TO CHANGE your
brain waves, a good place to start is with a song. Consider for a
moment the effect music has had on you in the past. I'm sure you
have experienced your mood suddenly lifting when you hear a
cheerful song on the radio. Perhaps the songs of your youth have
the power to transport you back to a simpler place in time. Or
maybe you have even been moved to tears by a grand symphony.

You may have even noticed that music can have an effect
on your body. Unconsciously your foot begins tapping or your
head bobs up and down in time to the rhythm. Occasionally, at
some moment when you feel unrestrained by the need to retain
personal decorum, you let loose and start dancing around the

room. These are magical moments, brief segments of time during which you are transported beyond the limits of your body into the much larger world of rhythm and movement.

In reality, when you respond to a piece of music, nothing actually changes in the world around you. Do you respond to a happy tune with a smile because that song somehow fixed all your problems? Of course not. Your life condition remains the same, with or without the song. But something did change— something within your brain—that allowed your perspective on life to change as well.

Dancing with Energy

Did you know that I am a musician? I have not received training in the usual way, but I often play instruments during my lectures, including flutes, ocarinas, gongs, chimes, and other sorts of folk instruments.

As I play, I do not follow any written music, just what comes naturally to me through the flow of energy. During the experience, I am transported, and I hope the audience along with me, into the movement of the music itself. Even if I did know how to read music, I would not use it during the lectures. If I did have a piece of music sitting in front of me, part of my awareness would be on the printed page, not in the actual pure vibration of each individual note as it is played. The point of these demonstrations is to lose oneself in the music, letting go of all thought and judgment.

I like to demonstrate this for people because it also shows how to live in harmony with the flow of life, letting each note come as it will, without resistance or judgment. To me the difference between great musicians and ordinary ones lies not in how they play the music but in how they play with the music. Likewise, we must learn to play with the reality of our lives by living completely in the flow and rhythm of each moment, rather than trying to play it according to the precon- ceptions and restrictions of the past.

Many years ago, I developed a training method called *Dahn- mu*, which is meant to open people completely to this sort of universal rhythm. The word *dahn* refers to the basic, vital energy of life, and *mu* means "dance"; thus it could be called "energy dance" in English. In this practice, which is a form of Brain Wave Vibration, you are encouraged to let go of all limitations and simply follow the energy of the moment, letting the flow of energy move your body as it will.

Serendipitously, the word *mu* can also translate as "noth- ingness," which accurately describes the mental state experi- enced through Dahn-mu. The state of mu, or nothingness, is also achieved during Brain Wave Vibration when the mind is truly empty of thought, and you are able to simply follow the rhythms of life without hesitation. At this point, the boundaries of your body cease to exist, and you may experience a profound sense of oneness—first with the rhythms of your own body and ultimately with the universal rhythms of all life as your sense of physical separation fades away.

Through this sort of energy dance, you will find that your body moves in just the way that it needs to move. Your body will find motions and stretches that will open the flow of energy in your body in just the right way. Your entire body, the spinal column and all the peripheral nerves, all the blood vessels and all the muscles, will move in unison with your own internal rhythms. In this way, you become your body's own personal yoga instructor, creating movements that exactly fit your body's needs at that moment. Every part of your body will open to vital healing energy.

I believe that there is a direct parallel between the condition of your body and the condition of your brain. When you release the stiffness in your body, you are also creating flexibility in your brain. You become the instinctive, spontaneous healer of your own body and mind.

The Messages of Music

Teenagers understand instinctively that music affects the brain, and thus they often seek to define themselves through associations with certain musical styles. Unfortunately, the music they seek is not always what lifts them to higher states; more often they are drawn to music that resonates with their current state of consciousness. Just as they are drawn to other kids with similar levels of maturity, they are drawn to music that resonates with their current brain wave patterns. A dark, angst-ridden teen is likely to be drawn to similarly themed music, where a more happy-go-lucky type might be more inclined to upbeat pop tunes. The same is also true for adults, even if somewhat less obviously.

You can see the effect of music throughout the history of humanity. It is an element that appears in every human culture and thus is often called the "universal language." Music clearly possesses an uncanny ability to transform human consciousness. This is evident in the fact that music is an integral part of virtually every spiritual practice on Earth. It also has the power to transform cultures.

A relatively recent example is rock and roll, which brought dramatic social change with it. At the time, people who supported the status quo reacted strongly against the music, sensing the inherent, almost primal power that it contains. In a way, Brain Wave Vibration works similarly to music like this, its rhythms opening the mind to new experiences and ideas.

Music seems to possess a remarkable ability to penetrate the human consciousness, even when nothing else can. One study of severely autistic young adults showed that music therapy was one of the few ways to improve their verbal, social, and behavioral performance.

Concetta Tomaino, a pioneer of music therapy, described her first job working with advanced dementia patients:

Half of the people were catatonic, and the other half
were so agitated that they had to have their hands tied
so they wouldn't pull out their nasogastric tubes. In my
very first session, I started singing "Let Me Call You
Sweetheart." The catatonic people opened their eyes,
the agitated people calmed down, and half of them started to sing along with me.

Since that time, Tomaino has devoted herself to uncovering the healing aspects of music at the Institute for Music and
Neurologic Function in New York City.

Brain Wave Vibration is a rhythmical activity that I have
seen reach the unreachable, as was the case for Anna Contreras.
Her daughter suffers from Rett syndrome, a genetic disorder
that prevents children from developing normally. Usually, these
children remain at the developmental level of a two-year-old and
display social skills similar to severely autistic people. Anna was
at the end of her rope. Her daughter was nineteen, yet she still
wore diapers and could not walk. Anna herself had experienced
many benefits from Brain Wave Vibration practice, so she began to wonder if it could help her daughter. The only problem
was that the girl could not even understand the concept of Brain
Wave Vibration, much less actually practice it.

So Anna decided to take things into her own hands—literally. Instead of expecting her daughter to do it herself, Anna
decided to rhythmically shake her daughter's body herself
with both hands. Anna and the doctors were amazed by the

progress her daughter made in only one short month. Both mother and daughter looked forward to this special time to connect, something that had been hard to achieve previously. The daughter's balance and motor skills improved drastically, and she smiles and interacts with people more than ever before.

The preceding are dramatic examples of people being awakened through music and rhythm. You may not have any of these sorts of problems, but, in a way, all of us need awakening of some sort. Most of us are stuck in a certain patterns of conscious awareness, and it is from these patterns that all our mental, physical, and spiritual problems arise. Brain Wave Vibration may be just the thing you need to jolt your body, mind, and spirit back to an awakened state of health.

The Healing Power of Rhythm

Brain Wave Vibration is a rhythmical training method; it begins with moving your body to the beat of music, and from there the sensation expands as you find your body's natural rhythm. In a sense, you could say you are calibrating your brain to get back in sync with your body.

People use rhythm instinctively to help calm their own brain waves. When a baby cries or fusses, what does a mother do? She rocks and gently bounces the baby until the baby quiets down. No one had to teach the mother how to do this;

she does so very naturally. Children will also rock and bounce on their own to calm themselves, if the parent is not there.

In Korea we teach children the *do-ri do-ri* movement, which is strikingly similar to basic Brain Wave Vibration. The child rocks the head side to side and repeats, "Do-ri do-ri, do-ri do-ri," which translates as "truth" or "principle." Because many energy pathways meet at the neck, it is thought to advance children's development, especially brain development.

Even as adults, we tend to bounce our knees and drum our fingers when stressed or nervous. Also, when we feel disappointment or disgust, we shake our head side to side. This movement is done around the world, which Charles Darwin noticed long ago through his observations of emotional expression. I believe these motions are instinctive because they help calm the brain waves in a natural way. Through the rhythmic movements of Brain Wave Vibration, I hope you will apply these methods to yourself in a more conscious, deliberate manner.

The healing power of rhythm is becoming clear. Recently, drumming has become an increasingly popular form of therapy and drum circles have become a popular pastime for people looking to relax and have fun. Activities like these seems to offer troubled individuals a chance to release stored emotions and to gain a feeling of personal power. One study found that workers who got together to participate in group drumming gained a much more positive outlook about their work and developed a sense of community with their coworkers. Researchers concluded that drumming circles provided a great release for the workers' stress and that the practice could reduce worker burn-out significantly, leading to a reduction in the rate of employee turnover (Stevens).

Drumming as therapy has been especially successful for psychological healing, particularly as a treatment for drug addiction. Researcher Michael Winkelman surveyed a number of drumming-based addiction treatments and found them to be overwhelmingly effective. According to his report, participants enjoyed drumming much more than any other form of treatment they had experienced previously, and they were much less likely to return to drug use after the therapy had ended. In addition to addiction recovery, the drummers were found to have improved social and psychological life coping skills, as well. Winkelman attributes these positive effects in part to the effect of the rhythms on the individuals' brain waves. Drum beats, he says, induce alpha and theta waves, and thus they help return the human body and brain to a state of relaxation.

When people go out to a nightclub or blast the latest pop tunes from their car stereos, they are, in a sense, self-medicating their own brain waves. Typically, these songs have heavy beats that allow the brain to settle down to a more primitive, prerational state of being, in much the same way that tribal drumming helps produce subconscious, trancelike states in indigenous healing practices. Of course, the effects are not quite so dramatic, but the constant, heavy beat does help the brain to "simmer down," escaping from the constant left-brain, prefrontal cortex activity that modern life demands. So the next time you see the guy in the car next to you bobbing his head up and down to the rhythm of the latest top-ten hit, you can think to yourself, "Oh! He knows Brain Wave Vibration, too!"

In his book *This Is Your Brain on Music*, neuroscientist and musician Daniel J. Levitin discusses the effect music has on the human brain. He notes that music is unique in its ability to stimulate all areas of the brain at once. He says, "Musical activity involves nearly every region of the brain that we know about, and nearly every neural subsystem." Thus, music is the ultimate brain activation exercise.

Music may be a great way to get the whole brain acting together as one. In my five-step Brain Education method, the goal of the fourth step, Brain Integrating, is to unify the three layers of the brain—the primitive brain stem, the emotional limbic system, and the rational neocortex. Very often one part of the brain undermines another, as when rational thinking is overcome by emotion. For example, fear may motivate someone to make an irrational decision, or the rational mind may suppress the full expression of emotion.

The goal of Brain Integrating is to get the various parts of the brain working together harmoniously, rather than competing with each other. Since it activates diverse parts of the brain, music seems to be a good step in that direction, which may also explain the cognitive advantage that children who study music seem to have over their nonmusical peers (Levitin).

Yull-yo, the Rhythm of Life

When I train people in the Brain Wave Vibration method, I usually use *sa-mul-no-ri*, the traditional drumming art of my native Korea. It has its roots in ancient aspects of Korean culture, originating in the rituals of farmers who wished to ensure the success of their crops.

The four *sa-mul-no-ri* instruments each represent a different weather condition: the *jang-gu*, an hourglass-shaped drum, represents rain; the *kkwaeng-gwa-ri*, a small gong, represents thunder; the *jing*, the larger of two gongs, represents the wind; and the *buk*, a large bass drum, represents clouds. The instruments are also thought to signify the voices of both heaven and Earth. The *buk* and *jang-gu*, which are made of leather, represent the sounds of the Earth, while the *jing* and *kkwaeng-gwa-ri*, made of metal, represent the sounds of the heavens. The music is composed to match the progression of nature—the wind blows, the clouds gather, thunder and lightning strike, and the rain falls. On hearing the music, listeners are swept up in the cycle of Earth's natural rhythms.

I believe that this music, like a lot of other traditional musical forms, possesses a remarkable ability to affect the brain positively. It may be that rhythmic music has a great psychological effect because the first experiences we perceive with our brains are rhythmical. Perhaps our ancient forbearers, being also more in touch with nature, were more aware of this human trait.

Medical science has confirmed that infants begin responding to sounds around them long before they are born (Shahidullah). When you were developing in your mother's womb, your ears were practically the only sensory organs taking in information. Perhaps your skin could sense the warmth of your mother's body, but it was a consistent, unvarying temperature, and you were suspended in the amniotic fluid, an environment with very little variety of texture. Your eyes were closed to the dark interior of your mother's body, and your mouth had no food to taste.

You lived alone in a dark world where the unceasing rhythm of your mother's heartbeat was your constant companion. This and the sounds of your parent's voices were the first stimuli to create connections in your brain, giving definition to your being. When you were born, the sounds of your parents' heartbeat continued to calm and sooth you. When you hear the sound of rhythmic drumming now, or when you follow the movements of Brain Wave Vibration, you are transported back to a place of newness and simplicity.

Music is such a consistent part of the experience of life that you could say that rhythm is essential to life. Medieval scholars of Europe hypothesized that a great harmonic system, called "the music of the spheres," kept the planets in their proper orbit and rotation. Likewise, they believed that an internal harmony existed within the human body. This may seem naïve to the modern scientific mind, but on an intuitive level, there is great truth in that concept. Just stop and quiet yourself for a moment, and you will feel it. Music really is a universal experience and the universal language.

When you return to this basic rhythm of life, you return to what I call *Yull-yo*, the never-ending rhythm that pervades all of life and the entire universe. Eventually, as you progress in your practice of Brain Wave Vibration, you should not rely on the music playing in the CD player, the music outside yourself. That music is just a reminder. Rather, you should go deep into the beautiful harmony that is part of who you are, a place one and the same as the entire universe.

CHAPTER 3

The Secret of the Brain Stem

Health is the thing that makes you feel that now is the best time of the year.

—Franklin Pierce Adams, columnist

E VEN AS A SMALL CHILD, you wit-
nessed the healing power of your brain stem at work. If you
scraped your knee, you could watch day by day as your body
repaired itself, eventually becoming a brand-new patch of skin.
This kind of phenomenon, although commonplace, is really
quite miraculous.

But what does the brain stem have to do with all this? Your
brain stem is like a hidden conductor of the great symphony
that makes up the intricate systems of your body. Without any
conscious direction from you, it sends out messages to the
body, telling your heart how fast to beat, commanding your
white blood cells to spring into action, directing your digestive

system to go to work, and coordinating a myriad of other bodily functions that continuously support your health and well-being.

The brain stem's role is essentially to maintain your state of equilibrium. The body is designed to maintain a consistent state of health. You could say that any prolonged disease represents lack of equilibrium in the body.

So then why do things sometimes break down? Occasionally it is because of invaders, like viruses and bacteria, that the body is just not equipped to face. But, as you know, this is not the scenario that most people in modern society face. Humanity has learned a lot about controlling these invaders.

The great majority of the diseases of modern society, as you probably already know, are the result of lifestyle rather than some outside influence. In a way, through the choices we habitually make, we get in the way of our brain stem, and it never really has the chance to do its job.

A long time ago, Hippocrates said, "Everyone has a doctor within him or her; we just have to help it with its work." Brain Wave Vibration is one way to get out of the way so that a deeper level of healing can begin.

Living in the Age of Stress

You have probably heard many awful stories about the health conditions of the past—stories of plague, famine, and poverty.

We look back on these times with a sense of relief that these hardships are a thing of the past for most people, at least those living in the developed countries of the world.

Yet, even as we have escaped many of these horrors, we seem to have invented our own kind of epidemic, one brought about entirely through our own choices. It is the scourge called *stress*.

Stress has been linked to almost every illness of modern society. The list of associated diseases is staggering: heart disease, cancer, high blood pressure, asthma, lupus, rheumatoid arthritis, fibromyalgia...the list goes on and on. And on top of that, there are a host of negative habits associated with the stress response—activities people do to find artificial relief, habits that throw the body into further imbalance, including overeating, smoking, and excessive consumption of alcohol.

Why, if we have been able to conquer polio, smallpox, and other deadly contagions, have we not been able to conquer this thing called stress? The answer lies in how we relate to the world from the inside out, not in how the outside world relates to us. When a doctor controls a bacterial infection with an antibiotic, he or she is attacking an invader that came from outside the body. But in the case of stress, the effects are largely self-inflicted.

It would be nice if we could simply eliminate stress in our lives with a pill, but that is not the reality. Nor is it likely that you will reach a point where you have fixed all of your problems and have no challenging situations to face. You may say that people or events in your life are stressful, but actually stress is something you yourself generate within your own mind. Controlling the effects of stress will require understanding yourself better, not changing your outside environment.

Consider, for example, two young men taking a graduate school entrance exam. Imagine they are taking the same exam and that both are equally prepared, but one person arrives at the classroom with sweaty palms and a racing heartbeat, while the other remains perfectly calm and relaxed. What really makes the difference here?

The distinction lies in the story that each student is telling himself. One may be saying to himself, "I will just do my best. Everything will be fine." Meanwhile the other is saying, "I am terrible at standardized tests, and my whole future depends on this one test."

In both cases, the story is the creation of the prefrontal cortex, the part of the brain that analyzes and judges our environment. In the case of the stressed-out student, he is sending out a message that says, "Emergency! Sound the alarms!" The hypothalamus, sitting like a guard on top of the brain stem, hears the message and then relays it through hormonal and bioelectrical signals to the rest of the body. The sympathetic nervous system, also known as the fight-or-flight response, is activated—digestion is slowed, heartbeat is increased, and circulation is compromised, including in the brain.

Ironically, the student who put so much weight on the outcome of the test has done little to help himself succeed. A mild stress response may have helped him perform better, but in this case it is too extreme, and he is caught in a state of imbalance.

Stress in and of itself is not bad. The brain stem wants to create balance between the sympathetic nervous system, which produces the stress response, and the parasympathetic nervous system, which is in charge of the rest-and-digest response. When our bodies are kept in a constant state of imbalance, disease is the likely result.

The part we have control over is the prefrontal cortex, the thinking part of the brain. To put it simply, people today think too much. The thinking brain is constantly sending messages that keep our bodies in a state of alarm, and they never have ample time to recover. The trick is to quiet the thinking mind and gain control over the content it produces so that the brain stem has a chance to coordinate the equilibrium that it exists to create.

As you begin to practice Brain Wave Vibration, notice the kinds of stories you have been telling yourself. Think of the manifestations of stress in your life and try to discover their root. Maybe they show themselves physically through headaches, muscle tension, or even disease, or mentally through bad habits like nail-biting, mood swings, or overeating. Ask yourself what kind of mental story is connected to these manifestations— stories about your own insecurities, the shortcomings of other people, and the inadequacies of the world around you. When you can stop telling yourself the same negative stories over and over again, you will be able to face the challenges of your life with strength and courage.

Send a Love Letter to Your Cells

You may have been taught to believe that your genes determine what you will become. This can be especially disempowering when you hear that you may inherit the diseases of your parents and grandparents. However, a whole new line of thinking is emerging from biological science. Now biologists realize that genes are not the only players in the intercellular game that decides your personal health.

As it turns out, the membrane that surrounds the cell may be more important than genes in determining your state of health. The cell membrane senses and responds to the surrounding environment. In other words, it is the brain of the cell, receiving and interpreting messages from the body. But who talks to your cells on behalf of your body, telling them how to act? It is the same element that talks to your organs—telling your heart to beat and your lungs to breathe. It is your brain.

Energy is the language spoken by your body. You probably already know that your brain sends bioelectric signals to your organs and muscles through the nerve pathways in your body. But did you ever consider how your brain talks to your cells?

Not long ago, biologists believed that the cell membrane was relatively inconsequential, that it simply functioned as a containment system that absorbed nutrients and other chemical substances as needed. More recently, however, biologists have looked more carefully at how the cell membrane responds to its surrounding environment. Bruce Lipton, a biologist studying how the cell membrane works, claims that the cell interprets its environment not solely based on chemical information but also based on energetic information.

New discoveries about the cell membrane have led Lipton and other scientists to reconsider the ancient Asian concept of ki, which was once rejected as irrational. As it turns out, the energy emitted by your brain, your brain waves, may be crucial to the overall health of your cells.

Cellular health is critically important for your physical health because cells are the building blocks of your body. If your cells are not healthy, your body is like a building made of weak, disintegrated bricks.

Remember that all disease begins at the cellular level. All cancers, for example, begin with one mutated cell. When organs malfunction, this also begins at the cellular level. And the integrity of the cells that make up the artery walls plays a big role in cardiovascular disease.

Fortunately, healing also happens at the cellular level. Your body has an amazing ability to heal and grow itself, which is what Brain Wave Vibration is all about. Through it, you can learn to communicate positive, healing energy to your body.

Brain Wave Vibration training helps synchronize your brain waves with the natural healing power contained within every cell of your body. You can start by making sure that the content of your thoughts is positive. Many studies have shown the important role of emotions and attitude in determining long-term health. Positive thinking patterns are clearly a precursor to good health. In addition, they help facilitate proper flow of ki through the body, leading to a vital, fully developed sense of health and well-being. Quantum physics has taught us that everything in the universe is ultimately energy, and Brain Wave Vibration empowers you to use your brain stem to emanate positive, supportive energy throughout your body and into your life.

Energy Management Is Life Management

Brain Wave Vibration is essentially a way of managing your energy, in much the same way that you manage your time or your finances. If you feel stressed out or burned out, you may think it is because you have too much to do. That may indeed be the case, but for most people, burnout comes from the inability to manage their energy, not from having too much to do.

Research has shown that the body and mind function according to ultradian rhythms, cycles in which the body moves from high-energy to low-energy states. At the low point of the cycle, which occurs every 90 to 120 minutes, your energy dips and your mind wanders (Schwartz). In response to this energy deficit, people usually reach for that extra cup of coffee, grab a sugary snack, or just suffer through the feeling of listless fatigue. This kind of habitual behavior in the long run only produces burnout and inefficient working habits. What people really need is an effective way to recharge their energy, rather than to push themselves artificially through the feeling of exhaustion and brain fog.

On top of this tendency, most people's work is not balanced from the brain's point of view. These days, most people find that their jobs require a great deal of processing from the prefrontal cortex, especially for left-brain functions, like logical, symbolic, and verbal processing.

Brain Wave Vibration can function as a kind of energetic and creative battery charger for your body and brain. Whenever you find yourself in that energetic valley, or when you feel blocked creatively, use the method to bring new life to your day. By doing so, you are shaking loose the tension that has built up in your body, and you are opening your body to new energy. Furthermore, as you quiet your thinking mind, you give the creative right brain a chance to chime in, allowing new opportunities for innovative ideas and solutions.

According to Asian traditional medical models, we all have meridians that run through the body and carry life energy, known as *ki*. According to this model, any pain or disease that occurs in the body is the result of blockage to that energy flow. Acupuncture, a method whose efficacy has been well established in several studies, seeks to improve the flow of energy, fine-tuning it for optimal health. Many mind–body practices, like tai chi and yoga, also help open up these pathways. Likewise, Brain Wave Vibration allows you to shake loose the blockages in your body for better energy flow.

A New Definition of Health

Our current approaches to health care have done much to extend our life span, but our health span may not be so impressive. American men, for example, can expect to experience some kind of debilitating illness by the time they reach age sixty-seven, and women can expect to experience the same by age seventy-one (World Health Organization). Thus, you can expect to spend most of the last decade of your life in ill health.

I firmly believe that this is not the way it should be. A friend of mine, named Kwan-sik Min, is a good example of how I think we should live. Mr. Min, who served as a minister of education in Korea before his retirement, was the picture of good health to the day of his death at age eighty-nine.

Despite of his advanced years, he never gave up his active lifestyle, sustaining a full schedule of speaking engagements and leisurely sports activities. One key habit, I think, was that he walked regularly, and always with a spring in his step. His gait and demeanor were so youthful that he soon garnered the nickname Forever-Young Brother. On the day he died, he played a game of tennis in the morning, had a full lunch, lay down for a nap, and then gently passed away in his sleep.

The time has come to mix the wisdom of East and West to get the most out of life. Scientists have set the human life span at 120 years, yet few of us live even two-thirds of that in good health. The pharmaceuticals and medical technology we have are amazing, but to live life fully we must rediscover some of the old wisdom that connects us more intimately with our own bodies. Western medicine has many gifts to offer, but the old systems, based sometimes on hundreds of years of human experience, should not be dismissed out of hand.

When thinking about the definition of health, we should think about more than just the mechanical functionality of our bodies. We should consider the quality of our actual being and the content of our moment-by-moment experience. Our technological society has, in many ways, given us a more comfortable existence, but it has also separated us from ourselves. The key is to evaluate the invisible energetic element that cannot be so easily assessed by scientific investigation, but that has been understood intuitively by many generations of people across the cultures of the world.

The difference between Mr. Min and most people his age is not the superiority of his biological functions but the energetic spirit with which he lived. Essentially, he learned to manage his energy effectively.

Our lifestyle today could be likened to a yo-yo that is continuously on the move, up and down, over and over again. If you have played with a yo-yo much, you know that after a certain amount of time the string becomes kinked and the yo-yo no longer runs smoothly. Every once in a while, you have to stop and let the string unwind. Think of Brain Wave Vibration as a way for you to stop the constant movement of your mind to let it untwist and become whole again.

Make Peace with Your Brain Stem

The history of humanity has been a constant progression toward the limits of rational thought. Through our ability to judge, analyze, and plan, we have gone a long way toward controlling the vagaries of human existence. In some ways we have tamed the uncontrollable, mysterious aspects of life on this planet. In doing so, however, we have introduced imbalance, both in our own personal lives and on the planet. The effect of imbalance on the Earth is becoming obvious, and the effects on our health are becoming clear as well.

Modern life essentially puts us each at war with our own brain stem, as we suppress the prerational, subconscious side of ourselves in favor of rationalistic obsession. Our educational system currently favors those whose gifts are in analytic, left-brain activities, like reading and mathematics. Psychologists acknowledge that there are many forms of intelligence, including interpersonal, emotional, and creative intelligence, but these are not the talents that usually earn the accolades. We do not educate the whole brain; rather, we develop and reward the prefrontal cortex nearly to the point of excluding the rest. The same continues throughout life as cognitive-based skills usually earn greater money and status within society.

Of course, the other parts of the brain keep working for us, but we do not educate ourselves to use them well. The thinking mind has become so central to our lives that it often carries

[**Layers of the brain**]

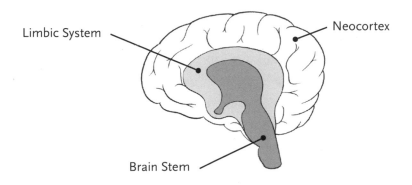

Brain Wave Vibration is meant to help the brain's
various functions work together in harmony.

us away from ourselves into patterns of negativity. Constantly
judging everything that comes our way, we send our bodies into
a state of continual alarm and lack of equilibrium.

It is something of an oversimplification, but it can be helpful to think of the brain as having three layers. They are the
brain stem, which controls the body's unconscious and reflexive functions, the limbic system, which is involved in emotional
response and memory, and the neocortex, which controls the
"higher functions" of the brain, such as motor commands and
conscious thought. All three "layers" constantly work together

as the conductors of our internal and external, conscious and subconscious experiences of life.

Brain Wave Vibration, like other forms of Brain Education, differs from most other educational methods in that it seeks to educate all three levels of the brain. Our current educational system usually only focuses on the top level of the brain by emphasizing rational thinking, language development, and mathematical skill. In my experience with people, I have concluded that people's health and happiness are greatly compromised if they have a busy head full of facts and figures but no tools to help them integrate their "thinking brains" with the emotional and subconscious brain.

Most educators already acknowledge that there are many kinds of intelligence. But for the most part, our society rewards intelligence that arises from the prefrontal cortex, the part of the brain that governs "executive functions," like decision making and rational thought. The content of the SAT Reasoning Test, which as you know can be a make-or-break exam for young adults of college age, focuses entirely on prefrontal skills like math, reading, and critical thinking, a good reflection of our preference for this type of intelligence.

Psychologist Matthew Kelly refers to another kind of intelligence he calls "psychophysiological intelligence," which essentially is the sort of intelligence that we have within our own body, waiting to help return us to a healthy state of balance. This type of intelligence is rarely acknowledged because it is not guided consciously by our thinking brain. However, this kind of intelligence can be seen every day, as our brains carry out the commands that keep our bodies healthy and functioning.

Through Brain Education methods like Brain Wave Vibration, I am interested in uncovering and maximizing this sort of intelligence. This is not to say that other sorts of intelligence are not important. All the many abilities of the human brain are important, and it makes sense to do our best to educate the entire brain for maximum efficiency. But is it really possible to educate people to control even subconscious responses? Can we develop psychophysiological intelligence the way we develop language or mathematical skills? I believe we can.

An example of this kind of education is meditation, which is essentially the practice of slowing, or even stopping, the chaotic chatter of the mind to find a deeply focused, highly aware state. Many recent studies have shown the beneficial effects of meditation, which gives our brain a much-needed rest from the mental patterns that keep us stressed. Thinking is not necessarily bad, but at times we need to find ways to move beyond our typical modes of thinking, for our own health and for the health of those around us.

In 2003, the popular magazine *Psychology Today* reported on a study completed by Jon Kabat-Zinn, Ph.D., at the University of Massachusetts. In that study, Zinn measures the brain waves of forty-one high-powered and highly stressed employees at a high-tech firm in Madison, Wisconsin. Twenty-five of these people were trained in the art of meditation, while the other sixteen were left untrained as a control group. After eight weeks, the meditators' brain wave activity had shifted from the right hemisphere to the left hemisphere. As this shift might suggest, the meditators reported that they felt significantly calmer and less stressed than before the training.

Essentially, these employees had received education to develop their psychophysiological intelligence, something that may have been completely missing from their previous educational experiences. It seems perfectly reasonable that this sort of thing should be a commonsense part of basic life-skill literacy. However, many people find the traditional practice of sitting silent and still in the lotus posture while trying to empty the mind to be very difficult. Even if they feel some results, many people give up after a short time of practice. Brain Wave Vibration, I believe, offers people similar results but is easier to practice. It could be called a moving meditation. Through the rhythmic, repetitive movements of Brain Wave Vibration, you may momentarily disrupt any stressful thinking patterns, creating a calmer state of mind. In addition, your body gains all the benefits that come through movement and vibration.

How Miracles Are Made

Miracles are really not so extraordinary. Actually, just the fact that all your bodily functions keep going as they do is a miracle in its own right. When we say something is miraculous, to me it only means that someone has managed to tap into a power that was already within his or her brain, waiting to be discovered.

One woman I know sustained an injury to her tailbone that caused her constant pain. She went to many doctors, but they told her the problem could not be fixed. She came to a Dahn Yoga center to practice Brain Wave Vibration, hoping she could find some relief. She was a doctor herself, a dentist, so she remained skeptical that she would ever find permanent relief. At best, she thought, she could lessen the pain to some degree. To her surprise, her pain completely disappeared after only three months of practice.

I am not telling you this story so you can be impressed with Brain Wave Vibration; it is a very simple activity that requires little effort. Rather, I am telling you this story so you can be impressed with the marvel of the human body. I believe this woman was able to heal because the subconscious part of her brain, the brain stem, already knew what it needed to do to create wholeness in her body; she just needed to get out of its way, which is what Brain Wave Vibration allows. The body contains a wonderful intelligence that surpasses our current understanding. This is the intelligence of the brain stem, a part of the brain that orchestrates things so complex that our thinking brain can only begin to grasp them.

You can begin to glimpse the source of miracles through the phenomenon called the placebo effect. As you may know, this effect occurs when healing seems to happen as the result of the patient's beliefs about a given treatment, rather than because of any actual mechanism brought on by the treatment itself. For example, a doctor might give a patient an inert sugar pill, but the patient may believe that they are receiving a powerful medication. Often the patient will feel better, simply because they believe that they are taking an effective medication. And, by the same token, if we believe that a given treatment will have a negative effect of some kind, if probably will, a phenomenon known as the "nocebo" effect.

Many researchers disregard the placebo effect as a false trick of the mind. However, there is no denying that the healing that occurs is to some degree real. Actual changes do take place in the body based on our beliefs. Researchers Moerman and Jonas coined the term "meaning response" to describe actual physical changes that happen in the body during treatment with placebo medications.

To me, the placebo effect suggests that the body, influenced by workings of the brain, possesses untapped abilities to heal itself. Perhaps we just need to learn how to get out of the way.

CHAPTER 4

The Source of Intention

Aerodynamically, the bumblebee shouldn't be able to fly,
but the bumblebee doesn't know it,
so it goes on flying anyway.

—Mary Kay Ash, founder of Mary Kay Cosmetics

You CAME INTO THIS WORLD wanting to be someone who makes things happen. From day one, you were a creation machine. You picked up objects in your tiny hands as soon as you could manage to grasp them. You fumbled them around in your hands, feeling their shape and texture, and even popped them in your mouth, wanting to know everything about the world around you.

As you gained knowledge of the world, you wanted to assert your influence over these objects. You pushed your bowl off the table, just to see it fall. You cooed and squealed, trying to understand the nature of your own voice. All your senses were open to discovering the living world around you.

This same drive eventually pushed you up through your own developmental process as you experimented with your body, and you eventually learned to walk and talk. All the while, magical events were happening in your brain—brain cells growing and connections developing.

As you grew older, you became more and more proficient at influencing the world around you. You earned money, gained status, and developed a solid sense of identity. But along with this came suffering and a yearning to go somewhere beyond this physical world. At some point, you may have asked, as I did, "What is this really all about?"

The problem with the physical world is that it is easy to forget what lies under the surface of things. When you were that infant exploring the world, you had just come into the world with a purpose. But the world of form distracted you, and you forgot, for a moment, who you really were.

The Human Predicament

It has often been observed that there are two selves within the human being. There is the self who is present in the surrounding world—interacting, doing, making, having—and then there is the self watching the self. The false self is a mask we wear for the world, a manufactured product of the ego. It is something we build on and construct throughout life to give ourselves a role to play in the world outside ourselves. The true self, on the other hand, is the higher you, the essential and unchanging part of you. It craves the highest forms of human interaction, such as unconditional love and harmonious unity with others. The struggles of life stem from lack of accord between these two selves, a predicament that arises from humanity's unique place in the universe.

You have probably noticed how vastly human behavior can differ, ranging from the person who gives all in service of others to the one who violently uses and abuses other people. Human beings are unique among the inhabitants of Earth because we are simultaneously Earthbound and divine, simultaneously Earth's people and heaven's people. Our upright stature—with our head in the sky and our feet on the ground—is a symbolic reminder of this.

The true self is the part of you that knows there is more to life than just the surface level of this world. It is the part of you that urges you to choose according to your highest self. However, through life we develop more and more attachment to this physical world, and the voice of the true self becomes muffled. Fortunately, we have been given the struggles and obstacles of life to help us remember who we are.

As a youngster, I was completely vexed by this predicament, but I had no way to solve it or to understand it. I could not concentrate, and my moods fluctuated wildly. I remember a conversation with my high school roommate, a straight-A student who my parents hoped would have a good influence on me.

He always sat studying at his desk, as soon he got home from school. One day, I sat there staring blankly at the back of his head as he studied.

"What are you doing?" I asked.

"Can't you see?! I'm studying," he replied.

"Why are you studying?" I asked.

"A quiz is coming up. I have to get good grades to get into a good college."

"Why do you want to go to college?"

"To be successful."

"What are you going to do after becoming successful?"

"Live happily."

"What is happiness?"

Finally, he turned around, perplexed by my question. Being the A student he was, he sincerely wanted to answer the question. He could not find an answer; he just stared at the ceiling.

"What is the purpose of our life?" I asked.

"Do you know?" he returned.

"I don't. That's why I am asking."

"Let's stop. There are so many other questions to solve."

"But everything hangs on the answer to this. It is the first thing to solve," I said.

Not too much later, my roommate requested to live in another dorm with someone else. It was no wonder, given my obsessive behavior and my brooding nature. Most of my peers avoided me, my grades suffered, and I had no sense of direction. At the time, it seemed as if these questions that occupied my mind were haunting me like a dark specter, but now I have come to see them as a gift that allowed me to really get to the underlying nature of life, in spite of the pain involved.

No one likes problems. Nevertheless, all of your problems are a blessing. They all exist to help you realize your true self.

When facing any problem, remember that the problem itself is just an illusion that stems from the false self created by the ego. Most people make the critical error of focusing on the problem itself, which ironically just brings more of the same into being. What really matters is not why or how the problem is happening but your relationship to the problem. One thing is definitely true—you will never be able to hate your problem out of existence. What really matters is your attitude about it. To upgrade your attitude, you must first consider how your brain is operating in relationship to the problem.

Upgrading Your Brain Operating System

I see the brain as similar, in some ways, to a computer. Granted, the brain is far more complex and can be modified through self-directed intention, which is certainly not the case with computers. However, I think it is a useful analogy to think in terms of the brain possessing an operating system.

Every brain, like every computer, has an operating system through which it processes the programs it receives. If you have not been able to create your life as you really want, then perhaps you simply can't run that program on your current brain operating system. To do so would be like trying to run a current computer program on a version of Windows from the 1980s.

Your operating system is the system of beliefs and preconceptions through which you interact with the world. Sometimes these beliefs are very helpful to us if they help us understand the world by helping us process the data that we constantly receive through our senses.

But sometimes our brain operating system is programmed in a way that does not suit our intentions for our life. For example, let's say you really would love to learn how to draw, but you have a belief about yourself that says, "I am not talented. Anything I try to draw is embarrassing." You can see how your intention, which is like a program you would like to run, is incompatible with your underlying belief about yourself, which is like your operating system.

The same is true for anything else that you wish to manifest in your life. If you want more money, upgrade your underlying beliefs about money. If you want better relationships, reevaluate how your brain processes relationships. This is true for anything you can dream of having or achieving.

Good information is key to programming the operating system to help you achieve health, happiness, and peace. For example, cancer patients are often told to visualize white blood cells as valiant knights on beautiful white steeds, coming to kill the enemy invader, the cancer cells. These patients are essentially bombarding their bodies with empowering thought that runs in opposition to the highly negative information that usually surrounds the word *cancer*. The same sort of concept can be applied to any problem or desire you have in your life. All you need is positive information and a way of processing that information that fully supports your intent.

Think of Brain Wave Vibration as a way of rebooting your computer, your brain. Choose the information you want to insert and think of it as a service pack, something that will help your brain operate in accord with your wishes.

If you look at the progress of your life so far, it will not be hard for you to figure out how your brain operating system might not be working compatibly with your dreams. It will be especially evident in any self-doubt or negative assumption you hold. As you practice Brain Wave Vibration, visualize yourself deleting these limitations and replacing them with completely positive, supportive beliefs.

I encourage you to set a truly marvelous goal for yourself. Don't choose something small and safe that you already know you can achieve without much of a problem. Rather, choose something that would amaze even you if you were to achieve it. Choose something that fills you with delight just to think about. If some part of you says, "But I could never do that," just dismiss it as some out-of-date part of your operating system that needs to be reprogrammed.

Of course, I know it is not so easy to set a grand goal. Like anything, it needs practice. You can practice by moving toward your big dream through small achievements. Like a marathoner, you need to run the first mile to run two miles. Eventually, you will reach the finish line.

But how do you know you have set the right goal? Joseph Campbell is famous for saying, "Follow your bliss." I think this applies here. If your goal makes you genuinely happy over the long term, it is probably in accord with your true self and therefore will be genuinely satisfying to you. Since the true self thrives on service to others, rather than to self, you will probably find some goal that will do amazing feats to heal and transform humanity and the world.

The brain has the remarkable power to produce results according to its master's intention. That is why it is important to use the brain only for causes that are productive, creative, and peaceful. If the brain only works for the ego's satisfaction, no matter how productive or creative it might be, it will make your life miserable—you will never have peace. That is why setting the right goal becomes crucial.

Rebooting Your Brain Operating System

If your brain's belief system is like an operating system, how do you keep it functioning well? After all, you can't go online to download an upgrade for your brain. But you do download information into your brain all the time. The trick is to be in charge of what you download. You want to be in charge of what songs are placed on your iPod, right? So why not demand the same for your brain? Here are three basic principles that can help keep your Brain Operating System (BOS) in top running condition:

1. Good news makes a good brain.

There is no way your BOS can function well if you feed it a steady diet of doom and gloom. No matter how tough things get, you must find a way to keep giving your brain hopeful information about yourself, your life, and the future. No good news? Then make some good news! If you can't find any good news, then you have truly been defeated by your negative information. Just look around you. If you open up your eyes wide enough you will see that you are surrounded by blessings. People tend to focus on the negative aspects of life, even when they are deeply blessed.

Don't wait for the network news to start broadcasting good news before you start looking for it yourself. And don't blame them for your negativity either. Right now, negative news is the world's addiction, and the reporters will continue to give us whatever best transfixes us as we sit there, mesmerized by the light of the cathode ray tube. The news on these shows will change when people change themselves and start making good news for themselves.

2. If you choose it, it will happen.

This statement is really not as magical as it sounds; it is quite commonsense. Consider, for example, the economy. When economists tell us that the economy is solid and growing, we spend and invest our money freely and without much worry. Through our spending, we stimulate the economy even more, thereby helping to fulfill the prophecy of experts. If they predict a downturn, and we believe it, then we will be more likely to spend cautiously and save more. Of course, there is no doubt that certain patterns of growth and decline will exist independently of our beliefs, but clearly our choices about how to act in the world can perpetuate events in one direction or another.

The same is also true about our lives. If we hold some belief about ourselves, we are likely to make decisions and actions that support that notion. For example, if you believe that you do not relate well to the opposite sex, you will probably create situations that confirm that belief. By the simple act of holding that belief in your brain, you will very likely be guarded in ways that would undermine any relationship, with the opposite sex or not. If you choose a different set of beliefs and responses, a different set of circumstances will arise.

Thus, it is important to believe unequivocally that you can have exactly what you want in life and make choices accordingly. If you want great relationships, choose to make that happen. If you want success in your career, get rid of the idea that roadblocks stand in your way and choose success. If you believe completely in your ability to choose your life's content, you already hold the golden ticket.

---

3. Always stay awake.

Information has a way of seeping into your consciousness, sometimes even without you knowing it. Because so many things in our culture are motivated by fear-based competition, there are a lot of people who would rather you not know about your true creative power. Many negative assumptions are fed to us from the earliest age, and most of us carry these around without ever stopping to evaluate the truth of those assumptions.

Being awake means being aware at all times of the information that is coming into your brain and being created by your brain. Your brain naturally wants to know more and more about the world, so it is anxious to gather information and to determine the truth about life. This in and of itself is a fine thing. However, one must gain both the wisdom and the humility to realize that a human being's perception of the world is always limited.

Much human strife, and even deadly warfare, has been created by the misconception that one belief system is better than another. In reality, all belief systems are constructed out of informational assumptions carried by particular individuals and groups of people. An awakened person is able to acknowledge the limitations of his or her own field or perception, and thus is able to accept, reject, or modify information. Through this awakening about the nature of information as it passes through the processing plant of the brain, you will be able to continually grow and expand your awareness, rather than locking it into preconceived patterns of limiting beliefs.

Matter Follows Mind

In Eastern thought, there is the saying "Where the mind goes, energy follows." In other words, energy travels exactly where your mind wants it to go. Everything we accomplish in this world begins with a conscious thought.

This is not as esoteric or magical as it might seem; it is just the commonsense way that things happen. For example, if you admire a tall building in the middle of a city, you can be certain that it all began in the mind of the architect working in tandem with the investors, contractors, and workers who brought it into being. As all these minds came together, energy began to flow toward the fulfillment of the vision. In that way, imagination became reality. Every space mission, every classic piece of art, every saintly act began as a thought in someone's mind.

You can think of your life as being a little like knitting. When you first begin, there is no shape to it, but you keep knitting with some goal in mind—to make a sweater, a sock, or whatever.

Every stitch is like a thought that you add to the overall shape of your life. Eventually, thoughts lead to action and the form will emerge, if you can only keep your intent in mind. If you have no clear vision, however, you will end up with a random pile of knotted yarn.

Everything I have achieved in my life happened one stitch at a time. I began with just one single student, and every step that followed was like a carefully placed stitch. Eventually, my plan began to emerge as a whole, just as a sweater takes form.

The key is to keep the big picture always in mind, even when it seems so far away. In my life, I have faced many moments that could have destroyed me. I could have gotten lost in the details of those events and become swept away by the emotions that accompany them. I have come to realize, however, that life situations, no matter how difficult, are only temporary.

You must remember that life is not a romantic movie. When you take a big step forward in life, it is not likely that anyone will be there to say, "Congratulations! You are so brave! Here is your reward." If you have someone that supportive in your life, that's great, but don't count on it. In fact, life sometimes dishes up exactly the opposite.

I remember arriving for the first time in the United States years ago. I landed at John F. Kennedy International Airport, hardly speaking a word of English, ready to experience a culture that was completely foreign to me. I planned to meet an instructor who was struggling to keep a center open in New York, so I had packed a few thousand dollars in my suitcase to assist him.

Shortly after I retrieved my bag from the baggage claim, I placed it on a cart and began to look for the person I was to meet. All of a sudden, a man was standing in front of me with his face close to mine, shouting something I didn't understand. All I knew how to say was "What?! What?!" Before I knew what was happening, I looked behind me and saw another man running down the corridor with my bag in his hand. Before I could think of what to do, both men had disappeared into the crowd.

To say the least, I was devastated. It seemed like such a harsh welcome to America. Many emotions came flooding over me. The easiest thing would have been to return with my student to Korea. First impressions are always very strong, and it was hard to resist negative information that my brain created to explain the situation. I could have concluded that America is a bad place or that this event was a bad omen. In troubled times, it is easy to fall for this way of thinking.

However, I decided that my greater goal was far bigger than this one temporary situation. So, I opted to change my information about the event. I decided not to think, "I was robbed when I came to America." I also did not want to think, "I have lost several thousand dollars." Instead I decided to think, "I made a donation to New York City." That way, I could be happy about the incident and move on toward the creation of my vision. And indeed, that "investment" did give rise to many great things, none of which would be possible if I had followed the negative thoughts and emotions that came with the initial event. Negative emotions are normal and natural in the face of life's challenges, but to be caught up in them is detrimental to the progress of life. Realize how quickly you can change your brainwaves, and always keep an eye on the greater vision of your life.

All you need is genuine determination to bring what you desire into reality. If you really want to start creating your life, get the word *impossible* out of your vocabulary. Yes, there is a certain value to remaining realistic, but do you really desire much beyond the realm of realism? I have met few people who honestly desire something that goes beyond the basic laws of the universe. I am willing to bet that everything you are looking to create will fit very nicely into the system of reality as it is currently manifested, so don't be afraid to go after what you want in life.

I don't believe in greatness that is bestowed as a rare gift to a few lucky ones. Rather, I think all people have greatness inside them. It is just a matter of persistence—sticking to what you have envisioned until it is reality. I have a deep conviction that everyone, including you, has been given exactly the right set of gifts to fulfill some magnificent purpose in life. Greatness must simply be chosen. And if you choose it, it will happen.

CHAPTER 5

Healing Informational Maladies

True genius resides in the capacity for evaluation of uncertain,
hazardous, and conflicting information.

—Winston Churchill, British prime minister

THE BRAIN IS ESSENTIALLY an infor-
mation processing machine. Thus, how we use our brains depends on how we use our information. By this standard, I
believe that many people today lack a certain level of brain health.
Their brains may look perfectly healthy on an MRI scan, but are
they processing information in healthy ways? If not, it is a serious
problem because we are living in the Information Age, where
information moves and can be gathered at an alarming rate. The
health of our culture depends on the informational health of our
brains. Fortunately, it is easy to identify and correct dysfunc-
tional informational processing.

The Three Diseases

Three main types of informational disease are prevalent today. I believe that these three "diseases" cause people to fail to achieve their true potential. These diseases are born out of habitual ways of thinking about ourselves and the world around us. For most of us, these diseases simply disrupt our relationships and undermine our dreams. At their worst, they lead to terrible conflict and violence in the world. If we can recognize and solve these fundamental problems, I believe we can create a better world, in addition to healthier, more satisfying lives.

One of the most common forms of informational disease is something I call **Information Immune Deficiency**. In this case, the brain loses the ability to filter out information that is destructive to ourselves or those around us. Any piece of information can be seen as a virus or bacteria, spreading from host to host. Some information is not harmful at all, while other information is quite damaging to the host. It is up to our brains to determine what information is helpful and what is harmful. If our brains fail to filter out harmful information, that information begins to grow inside of us, just as a cold or flu germ might. If allowed to replicate unchecked, that piece of information begins to weaken our entire brain, and those around us might also be affected.

As you know, information can be gathered easily these days. And, if you have spent any time at all searching the Internet, you know how damaging information can be. The Information Age makes it easy for bigotry and perversions of all kinds to gather and fester. Negative information abounds, waiting for some susceptible brain to give it a breeding ground.

Information is at the core of many of our society's most serious problems. Consider, for example, the problem of racial and cultural intolerance. When the brain succumbs to such things, it is succumbing to negative information about other people. If a person's brain is able to justify terrible acts of violence, then you can also be sure that something has corrupted that person's brain. However, you don't have to be a bigot or a terrorist to suffer from Information Immune Deficiency. The same malady in a milder form is at the root of so many of our basic personal problems, from the inability to sustain positive relationships to the failure to realize our personal goals and dreams.

Another common brain problem these days is something I call **Creative Paralysis**. You can see this clearly in individuals' inability to get outside their usual modes of behavior. When most people face a problem, they keep on returning to the same old response to that problem, never trying any solution that is the least bit creative. This is true on the global scale, where issues are dealt with in the same ineffective ways, as well as on the personal level, where the same old habitual responses keep people locked in unsatisfactory relationship and behavioral patterns. Why can't people break out of Creative Paralysis? Again, it is information—information that says, "This is the only right way of doing things."

The third common informational issue is called **Addictive Inertia**. In this case, we may recognize that better information is available to us, but we simply don't use it well because we are addicted to our old way of being. In physics, the word *inertia* refers to an object's resistance to a change in its state of motion. In other words, if you push a ball in a certain direction, it will continue rolling in that direction until a greater force pushes it in another direction.

The same is true of the human brain. When we become accustomed to certain information, it can be difficult to change that information, even when we know it is not healthy. A good example of that is the way that individuals respond to our current environmental and energy crisis. Many of us now know that our lifestyle is depleting the planet's resources, but the force of momentum created by the information we have about what constitutes a good standard of living keeps pushing us forward on the same road.

Information Management

Mastering your brain essentially means controlling the nature of information in your brain. You could almost think of information as food for your brain. Low-quality information is like junk food for the brain, while high-quality information is like highly nutritious, satisfying food. And just like the other functions of the body, the brain's health suffers greatly if it is fed a consistent diet of low-level information.

The situation with many people's information consumption is not unlike the situation with food consumption. First of all, there is simply too much information being served up. We are constantly bombarded with facts, theories, arguments, advertisements, images, noise—the list goes on. Our brains cannot handle all the extraneous information.

Information used to be held by an elite few, the scholars and rulers of a time gone by. But now there is an excess of information available for everyone. Every piece of information is like a calorie. The brain, which has a natural love for acquiring information, slurps up the information wherever it can be found. Soon the brain is overwhelmed by the vast amount of information entering it. Information in its own right is not bad, no more than food is bad. But too much is too much, especially when the quality is not good.

Like fast food, you can get a lot of information cheap these days. Your mind, like your body, gets heavy and clogged up quickly if you don't make good choices about what you feed it. Brain Wave Vibration is meant to help you stop processing information, almost like a temporary information fast, so that you can begin to take control of your information consumption. To determine your information nutrition level, ask yourself three basic questions:

1. Is the information I am receiving empowering to me?

No piece of information is worth having if it weakens you or detracts from your ability to realize your full potential. Throughout their lives, many people receive disempowering information, messages that tell them "You are not good enough," "You are not pretty enough," "You are not smart enough," and so forth. You must learn to view these beliefs as tragic pieces of misinformation that have given rise to disastrous results in the world. You must be willing to reject this kind of information, because if you believe any of it, even a smidgen of it, you have unconsciously allowed a destructive virus into your brain.

The worst is when you give yourself this information. Your brain will take you very seriously if you tell yourself that you are not good enough or that you are lacking in any way. It will live up to what you tell it you can do, so always give it clear and positive information about yourself. You can acknowledge that you have shortcomings to work on, but you should not think that your faults are a permanent part of who you are. When doing Brain Wave Vibration, imagine that you are shaking all of this kind of limiting information out of your brain.

2. Does this information help me grow and improve my life?

It is important to note that not all empowering information is beneficial. Empowering information may help your true self, or it may simply build your ego, which is the product of your false self. For example, I could say to you, "You are smarter and better than everyone else in the world." That is indeed empowering information. However, you can see how it is not information that will help you grow and improve yourself. You must be wary of the ego as you choose information because it can mislead you easily, even causing you to be offended by empowering information that will help you achieve your highest self. Disregard information that does not propel you toward your highest self. Learn to differentiate that which contributes to your true self from that which appeals only to the egoistic self.

Another tendency of the ego is to collect information just for the sake of stockpiling an impressive array of knowledge. Knowledge can be a helpful tool, but hoarding it only clouds the mind and distracts you from your highest intentions.

3. Is this information truthful?

The most important point is to assess the truth or falsehood of the information you receive. As you advance in your ability to tap into the vibrations of the universe, you will also gain natural ability to discern right from wrong and truth from falsehood. You will learn to trust your intuitive feelings in this regard. When something feels right, you will know it is right. When it is in accord with your true self, you will recognize it as truth; when it is not, you will also recognize that. If in doubt, just ask your brain—not the thinking brain but the intuitive brain. It always knows and is ready to share its wisdom.

I believe that there is a link between disease and the health of our brain waves, and the health of our brain waves is determined by the quality of information we possess. It is possible that specific diseases, like cancer, high blood pressure, and diabetes, all relate to particular thought patterns. If you can change the brain waves that are producing the disease, then perhaps you can heal the disease as well.

One student of mine was a reporter, and he was constantly bombarded with negative information because he was in charge of reporting all sorts of negative news—accidents, crime, and the like. He was soon plagued with health problems, including deep fatigue and unnatural hair loss. On top of that, he smoked and drank too much to relieve the stress. Now his health has improved because he uses Brain Wave Vibration to clear away the negative information from his mind.

Fortunately, your brain waves can respond to positive information quickly. The body, by contrast, may take quite a while to recover from poor nutrition, if it can recover at all. You have seen the brain's resiliency if you have ever seen your mood change rapidly. You may have been having a terrible day and feeling very sullen, when all of a sudden some piece of positive information—maybe an upbeat song, good news from a friend, a child's smile—turns everything around for you. Part of the message of Brain Wave Vibration, however, is that you don't have to wait for these special moments. It is remarkably simple to choose the quality of information entering your brain and to control the resulting health of your brain waves.

The Three Cures

The good news is that informational maladies are really easy to cure, unlike physical illnesses. And unlike the body, which takes considerable time to heal, information can change instantaneously if the mind and heart are open. Fortunately, there are three "medicines" that can help people change their information: music, message, and action.

Music is the first informational medicine. As I mentioned before, all of us have had the experience of a song changing our mood. In a way, you could say that music is a kind of Brain Wave Vibration in its own right. Sound, after all, is vibration, and good musicians have the ability to organize these vibrations in a way that is especially effective for the human brain.

Of course, most musicians are not consciously attempting to influence people's brains, but when they are successful, that is precisely what they do. When a piece of music is called a "hit," what makes it a hit? From my point of view, something about the combination of rhythm, melody, and lyrics really resonates with the brains within a certain time and place in history. You could say that that musician "tapped in" to the vibratory brain frequencies that surround him or her. Thus, music often reflects the particular cultural and political condition of the society in which it was produced.

Sometimes, music is able to exceed the limits of generational preference and continue inspiring people for many decades, if not centuries. For example, the classical works of composers like Bach, Beethoven, and Mozart continue to resonate deeply with people. Even in the highly generational world of popular music, a few musicians are remembered as cultural icons while others are forgotten as "one-hit-wonders." For example, a recent survey was conducted asking people who their favorite rock and roll artists are. The choices differed greatly according to generation, reflecting the vast changes in style that had taken place over the years, yet people in their twenties, thirties, forties, fifties, and sixties all agreed that the Beatles were and are one of the greatest rock bands of all time (Luerssen). Artistic longevity of this sort, whether Mozart or the Beatles, represents music's basic, almost primal influence on the human brain.

People often refer to music as the "universal language" for its ability to move people in ways that defy the limitations of language and culture. In fact, brain scientists are confirming that language and music are processed in very much the same way in the brain, using the same structural areas of the brain and firing neurons in a similar pattern (Patel). It could be argued that language is indeed a sort of music to which we have ascribed very particular rules of grammar, syntax, and meaning. Music, then, could be viewed as a purer, more fundamental form of language, speaking directly to the mind of the listener without the need for precise meaning and interpretation.

While we are all influenced by music, I am not sure that we pay enough attention to the significant power it has over the human brain. Sometime when you have a little time on your hands, try to really feel the effect that music has on your body and mind. Lie down, close your eyes, turn up the volume, and feel the effect of the music. Feel its vibrations rolling over the surface of your body and penetrating into your cells; notice the images and sensations it brings to your brain. Music has unparalleled power to open up your mind and heart, thus it is critically important to surround yourself with positive, uplifting music.

If a piece of music has lyrics, it will also carry some kind of **message**, which is the second type of informational remedy. While music is an especially effective way to deliver a message, messages actually surround us in many different forms. Sometimes they are presented to us in a very straightforward way, as in a lecture or sermon. But messages also reach us in more subtle forms, such as through advertisement imagery or in the gestures we use to express emotion.

Messages can be either healthy or unhealthy, depending on

how they affect people and their interactions with others. To determine the relative health of a given message, you might try giving it what I call the "HSP Test." HSP stands for health, smiles, and peace. You can ask whether a message, in whatever form it presented, creates HSP in the world. Does this message create health, smiles, and peace? If you are sure that it does, then you can be sure that it is a healthy message that will help produce healthy information in people's brains.

Sadly, we are so used to being surrounded by unhealthy messages that we don't even recognize them as unhealthy. Sometimes these messages are delivered in nice, attractive packaging, so they may be difficult to recognize. Recently, I saw a television commercial that demonstrated how unhealthy messages can be delivered in attractive wrapping.

In this particular advertisement, a preteen boy and his friends declare how "cool" the mother is for serving a particular brand of fruit punch. On the surface, the situation appeared very sweet and cute, but the underlying message of the ad seemed to be, "Buy this sugary drink, and you will be a good mother who has the approval of your children." To apply the HSP Test, you might ask, "Does this message create health, happiness, and peace?" Clearly, the ad doesn't promote health when it falsely suggests that the consumption of sugary drinks is a good path to familial happiness. Secondly, it plays on a parent's desire to gain superficial approval (i.e. to be deemed "cool") from the child. In reality, of course, no junk food, video game, or name-brand sneakers will ever help us create strong, harmonious families, yet this sort of message is being delivered a thousand times a day.

Once we become more aware of unhealthy messages in our life, it becomes easier to simply ignore them. But that is not the end of the story. We must also find a healthy message to replace the unhealthy ones. The brain craves messages to help it make sense of this confusing world, and without a healthy message, the brain easily falls victim to the many unhealthy messages that surround it.

There is little you can do about the messages coming to you from other people. You will either accept them as true or not. But you can do something about the ones that you send. Whether you know it or not, you produce messages all the time, sending them to yourself and to those around you. Sometimes the messages we send are adopted or modified from other people's messages, and sometimes they are our own creation, but in the end it is our decision whether to pass them on to other people in our lives.

The messages you send to yourself are of primary importance because they, to a large extent, will determine how you function in the world. So begin by examining the messages you send to yourself and applying the "HSP Test." Do the things you tell yourself create health, happiness, and peace in your life? If not, modify your internal message to reflect the truly great being that you are.

Secondly, examine the messages that you send to other people around you. If you think you are a really nice person who rarely says an unkind word to anyone, look even closer. Look closely at the subtle gestures that communicate negatively to others. Think even about the content of your mind, for even un-spoken resentments and condescension can quickly undermine a relationship.

As hard as we try to be "nice" to others, it is of no use if our minds are still full of negativity toward others. Most of us are conditioned to compete with those around us, and thus we focus on their weaknesses and failings. The people around us are in-deed imperfect, but this is not all of who they are. Imagine how your relationships would transform if you chose instead to fo-cus on the best attributes people possess and on sending positive messages, through thought, word, and deed, that support the highest versions of all whom you encounter.

If you do not know how to deliver a message through words, try to deliver it through **action**. Action is the most important and most effective way to cure informational maladies, but sadly it is the one people are least likely to employ. Through action, we not only change people's minds, we change the world.

Many spiritually inclined people mistake tolerance for inac-tion. Learning to peacefully accept the conditions we face does not mean we cannot or should not change them. I have always said that a prayer is great, but a plan is worth ten times the value of a prayer. Any action taken, however, is worth ten times the plan. If you want a better life, then take some action to make it. If you want a better world, then take some action to make it.

On my journey, I have met many like-minded people. They look at what I have created and wonder how I have managed to do so much. My secret is simple—I act. I don't hesitate. When something seems right, I do it. Many years ago when I went up into the mountains to train, I gained many insights about the nature of life. But I did not believe for a minute that those insights were the final goal. As far as I was concerned, if I didn't put those awakenings into action in some way, they were meaningless.

It is a lot less risky to dream than to act. But as I often say, "No action, no creation." If we don't take decided action to create what we dream, we will never have our dream. Your head may be full of the best ideas ever conceived by humankind, but they will never have the slightest effect on the world if you aren't willing to step out of your routine and act.

Ironically, the most important time to act is when it is most difficult to do so. Sometimes, when people try to act upon their dreams, they find that the world is not necessarily receptive to them. They face opposition, criticism, rejection, and downright failure. Some people seem to scare themselves off from taking action, afraid of the consequences. Yet it is just this sort of fear that keeps the world as it is and people's lives stuck in ineffectual patterns. In the end, it is far better to have made an attempt and to have failed than to make no attempt at all. And even better than that is to keep trying, even when failure comes.

Information Transformation

All brains are good brains. However, information can affect the brain in ways that can distort its functioning. When negative information has taken over the natural workings of the brain, you could say that a good brain has become a bad brain. The brain naturally distinguishes positive information from negative, but sometimes we simply lose trust in our brain, allowing outside information to run the show.

You could say that a bad brain continually interprets the experiences of life in ways that undermine the inherent greatness within itself and other brains around it. A good brain, by contrast, can find positive, proactive ways to function in virtually every situation.

You may wonder how it is possible to stay positive. After all, doesn't life bring with it some awfully difficult situations? Certainly it does. I am not saying that everything in life should be sugar-coated or that anything negative that happens in your life is somehow your brain's fault. Rather, I am suggesting that you develop the habit of a positive viewpoint, as a kind of proactive default mode for your brain. This way, you will never feel defeated by the situations you encounter, and you will always have hope of finding a constructive solution to your problem.

Really, it is just a matter of how you construct your beliefs about a given situation in your head. You can develop the habit of turning something negative into a positive possibility by making small changes in how you view that situation. Consider the following pairs of statements:

"I can't do it."
→ *"I'll do my best."*

"People make me so angry."
→ *"I understand that everyone is growing and learning."*

"I feel so guilty about how that turned out."
→ *"I'll do better next time."*

"I am so frustrated by this situation."
→ *"I am determined to change this situation."*

"I have so many problems in my life."
→ *"I am grateful for all the challenges that will help me grow."*

"I am so worried about how things might turn out."
→ *"I have great hope for the future."*

The statements above the italicized ones are typical of how people view certain situations in their lives. The especially sad thing about these statements is that they completely undermine the person's ability to make change in the situation. The italicized statements next to the arrows, however, could be used in the same contexts but with much better results.

Wouldn't it be nice if there was a simple switch in our brains that we could flip to change negative thinking to positive? Well, in a way, that switch does exist, but instead of being labeled "on" and "off," it is labeled "love" and "fear."

Love and fear are the two essential motivating factors that can activate the human brain. Think of any major event in your life and consider what sort of human emotion underlies it. If you peel back the layers far enough, you will always see that love and fear are under the surface of human action, from the events of your personal life to the events that dominate the headlines.

When you are developing your beliefs about yourself and the world, you can use your love/fear switch. Examine the interior dialog you have in your mind, and see which way the lever is pulled. You can ask, "When I made this belief, was the switch turned to 'love' or 'fear'?" If you find that fear is in the background of any of your beliefs, you can flip the switch at any time. Or not. It is entirely up to you.

CHAPTER 6

Greatness Resides in Your Brain

Keep away from people who belittle your ambitions. Small people always do that, but the really great make you feel that you too can become great.

—Mark Twain, writer

O<small>N MY COMPUTER</small>, I have photographs of two little boys, both about seven years of age. The pictures are very meaningful to me, although I don't know either boy. One shows the face of a chubby little boy smiling blithely at the camera, and the other shows a picture of a starving boy sitting on parched earth with a vulture lurking in the background. These are pictures that represent the imbalance we have created in the world, an imbalance that reflects the incomplete use of our brains.

All the problems in the world were created by the human brain, and within the human brain lie all the answers. To me, these photos are symbolic of the root causes of suffering in the world. If all human problems result from the human brain, they can also be solved by the brain. Imbalance in the world is a reflection of the imbalance within our bodies and brains.

Brain Mastery

The phrase *brain mastery* probably makes you think of something slightly different than what I mean by the term. Brain mastery does not mean being smart or being able to perform mental tricks. Rather, brain mastery is the ability to maintain a proper relationship between your brain and the outside world.

If you are a brain master, you have an almost uncanny ability to stay in the moment and not be swept away by thoughts and emotions. You can control your attitude and keep a positive mind-set, regardless of the situation. And most importantly, a master of the brain never loses hope, no matter how dark the situation gets.

I remember one time when I was a young man there was a bridge under which people threw a lot of garbage. The garbage just piled up week after week. People complained about the garbage, but no one ever did anything to change the situation.

So one day, I decided I would do something about the problem. I began to clear the garbage away, one piece at a time. When all the trash had been hauled away, I buried it in a hole that I had dug in the mountains. I then planted pumpkin seeds in the ground covering the trash. Soon, big, beautiful pumpkins were growing there.

This was a huge moment of discovery for me. It came at a moment when I felt truly hopeless about my life. In my early twenties, I had failed the college entrance exams three times. I realized that all I really needed was the opportunity to do something positive for people, and that something positive could even come from a pile of trash.

True brain mastery is the ability to see possibility, even where others see only trash. Those pumpkins grew so well precisely because the garbage had been there before; the trash added nutrients to the soil.

For real brain mastery, you must learn to see your life in the same way, realizing that all the difficult, ugly parts of life can become the compost from which grows your own fulfillment. The trick is to keep a positive mind so that all the beautiful possibilities of life can be seen.

The Habit of Greatness

I now realize why that simple act of clearing the garbage felt so good. At that moment I glimpsed something in myself that I had not really seen before. Through that act, I, for a moment, realized my own greatness. I might not have described it as such at the time, but that is what it was. It was not an act that would get my name in history books, but it was an act that lifted me out of myself and onto a higher plain. Through that act, a discouraged and directionless young man stepped out of his sulking lower self to experience the egoless joy of the higher self.

True greatness is not really so difficult to achieve; it is simply a matter of determined contribution. But you may think, "I am not talented or smart enough to be someone great." I believe this kind of thinking is a delusion. Everyone has an inborn desire to contribute, and the ways in which one may contribute are inexhaustible. Greatness is just a matter of acting on that desire with unfailing conviction and determination. Everyone we describe as "great" has contributed something indelible to the development of mankind. This greatness can take all different forms and create different results in the world, but all these people have in common a drive to make a difference in the world.

Sometimes the great people of our history books do possess a particular gift to help them manifest their greatness. But most of all it is the determination to make a difference in the world that distinguishes them. Consider someone like Mother Theresa. Was she able to help so many on the streets of Calcutta because she had some special talent? Was it because she could sing and dance? Was it because she was more intelligent or more beautiful than other people? Mother Theresa, aside from her passion for helping others, was an ordinary person of ordinary means.

Scientists have looked at the brains of special people like Mother Theresa, as well as the brains of great artistic and intellectual geniuses, trying to find some anatomical differences to explain their unique qualities. While all brains contain certain unique attributes, there is no special "greatness" lobe of the brain that some are born with and others are not. Generally speaking, the brains of people we call "great" are the same as yours, with all the same basic abilities, some developed, others not.

Greatness is really born of habit, not of some predetermined genetic ability. Rather, greatness is something you cultivate; it is an attitude and an approach to life more than it is any sort of ability. In particular, it is an ability to face failure and keep on going anyway.

Consider, for example, Thomas Edison and his invention of the electric lightbulb. At that time, he was already a famous inventor, credited with an array of amazing discoveries. But newspapers of the day were especially interested in his work on the lightbulb because they knew, quite correctly, that such a device would revolutionize the way that people lived and worked.

There was one particular part of the lightbulb's development that proved very difficult, however. Edison could not find a filament material that would burn a sufficient amount of time. Everything he tried would just burn out after only a few seconds or minutes. He knew that he had to find a long-burning, inexpensive material or the lightbulb would simply not be practical.

Newspapers continued to report on the lightbulb's development, which began to be seen as something of a joke. Eventually, Edison had tried 2,000 different filaments, but to no avail. Reporters commemorated the event with a mock celebration of the failed lightbulb experiments in the papers. They were now treating Edison's search for a practical light bulb as little more than a pie-in-the-sky dream. One reporter teased Edison, asking, "So...how does it feel to have failed at something 2,000 times?" Edison replied, "Failed?! I haven't failed! I now know 2,000 ways *not* to make a lightbulb." And, of course, eventually he did find his answer.

This sort of response to obstacles is really what set Edison's brain apart from ordinary brains. It was not the size of his brain or his IQ but rather his determination that gave him greatness. While other people give up in the face of repeated failure, he just kept on going, determined to complete his goal. Edison himself once said, "If we all did the things we were capable of doing, we would all astound ourselves."

Whatever it is that you feel inspired to do in this life, realize that greatness already resides within your brain. It is just a matter of cultivating the mind-set of greatness. This means being willing to go outside of your comfort zone in pursuit of your goals. For most "ordinary" people, the tendency to shrink away from difficulties and potential failure is wired into the brain. To become great, you must rewire your brain with the tenacity and courage that is necessary for true greatness.

Rest assured that no one is born to be ordinary. Most of the connections you currently have in your brain got there through years of conditioning. If you are not living up to your true potential, it is only because you have had too much practice ignoring your greatness by continually choosing safe, limited ways of relating in the world. But if you really listen to yourself, I think you will hear a voice deep inside you saying, "Don't give up! You can do it!"

Through practice, you can rewire your brain for the habit of greatness. Neuroscientists tell us that the brain has a quality called "neuroplasticity," which allows it to continually reshape itself. In other words, our brains are not "hardwired" for any particular set of behaviors outside those that are instinctual or reflexive. Habits of any kind can be hard to change because these behaviors have become etched into our brains through years of repetition. Yet, we always have the power to change our brains, even in old age. Rewiring your brain for greatness is not all that different than changing any habit; through patience and commitment it can be done. It is not easy, because the voices of smallness and discouragement will inevitably pop up, as they are intrinsic to the habit of ordinariness. Brain Wave Vibration is here for you in those moments, allowing you to shake off those thoughts to begin again.

In a sense, living your greatness is a matter of self-respect. Stop waiting for someone to come around to tell you that you are great. I guarantee that no one will ever tell you that you are great until you do something to show that you are great. To be great you must act upon your greatness without any self-doubt. No one else can give you permission to do that. It is a decision you make all by yourself. If you want to be great, decide to be great now.

The Era of Greatness

While it is ultimately your decision to manifest your greatness, I would like to make a plea that you do so. The world desperately needs your greatness, and it needs it now.

As you know, the world has reached a real state of crisis. You are needed to help guide humanity to a better place, a place of increased health, happiness, and peace. Through your greatness, other people can also find their own greatness.

Just like an individual human being who is not living up to his or her potential, all of humanity is caught in certain destructive patterns of behavior that keep us locked in a perpetually imbalanced state. Some might say that this is the result of unchangeable aspects of human nature, but I disagree. This is a very pessimistic view of humanity that keeps us trapped where we are. Instead, I believe that human beings possess a natural desire and capacity for goodness.

In his book *Born to Be Good: The Science of a Meaningful Life*, psychology professor Dacher Keltner shows how our brains are intended for positive, meaningful interaction with other people. People who have a definite sense of purpose and a positive outlook on life have healthier brains. Brains thrive, he writes, when people have healthy relationships and a sense of contributing something of value to the world.

Even if you feel a little pessimistic about the current state of humanity, take a few moments to consider the people in your life. Would you say that the majority are doing the best they can to contribute positively in the world? It may be true that many are not living up to their full potential, but I bet that most want to do good in this world. Only a small minority of people are completely given over to the darkest aspects of human behavior. Most people genuinely want to contribute positively to the world, and it is only unfortunate habits based on fears about themselves and others that perpetuate people's negative behaviors.

For me, recovering our humanity is a matter of rediscovering our basic goodness. I call this the *hong-ik* spirit. In Korea, we use the phrase *hong-ik* to refer to a certain way of relating to the world that allows people to get beyond the individual worries and petty concerns of the individual self to consider the wider ramifications of our habitual actions. In Korean *hong-ik* means "wide benefit," referring to the ideal state of looking beyond individual desires to the collective needs of all humanity. Thousands of years ago, Korean culture used this hong-ik notion as the main foundation of its cultural identity. I think that other cultures also built their notions of civility on similar ideas, but somehow preference for individual happiness at the expense of the whole is more the norm these days, leading to the environmental and social injustices that we see all around us.

This is why your greatness is so important, now more than ever. True greatness is a matter of bringing love to places where hatred thrives, harmony where conflict prevails, and hope to places where despair constricts the heart. Real greatness means stepping beyond the petty concerns of the individual self to contribute to the whole of humanity. It will take courage and determination, but you can do it. When you do, you will experience the great joy that comes from restoring humanity's intrinsic sense of goodness.

If you are not sure about how to start living up to your greatness, just ask your brain. Even if your current situation seems insurmountable, sit quietly for a moment and hear the voice inside that is continually supporting you and providing encouragement. The greatest confidence is that which comes from within you, not from others' approval of you. Ask your brain, "Who am I really, deep down inside? What can I do to change this situation?" Within your brain lie all the answers.

CHAPTER 7

Tapping into the Infinite

The excitement of life is in the numinous experience wherein we are given to each other in that larger celebration of existence in which all things attain their highest expression, for the universe, by definition, is a single, gorgeous celebratory event.

—Thomas Berry, Catholic theologian

WE HAVE COME TO A POINT in human history where we need to redefine spirituality in a way that goes beyond religion—one that is satisfying to atheist and deist alike. Many of the squabbles we have today in regard to religious faith are not about spirituality at all. Rather, they are about layers of identity that we have piled on our spirituality. We keep trying to give specific form to something that is actually formless and beyond the limits of our rational minds. The more we try to define spirituality through theology and philosophy, the more it slips away from us.

I believe that spirituality is actually quite simple, so simple, in fact, that our rational minds will barely allow for it. Ironically, the tricky part is not learning to be spiritual. That part is automatic and requires little effort. The real trick is getting your thinking mind out of the way so that you can experience it directly and purely.

God and the Brain

There has been a lot of debate recently about the relationship between God and the brain. Some say that God is an outdated by-product of the brain, an illusion created by primitive parts of the brain. Others claim quite the opposite, saying that the brain contains evidence of a spiritual realm existing beyond the brain, which the brain is well designed to perceive.

One thing is clear to me: the brain is indeed designed for spiritual experience. It is also clear that such experience does not come from thinking long and hard about the minutiae of theological issues. Rather, it comes from a quieting of the thinking mind so that one may open up to the mysteries of experience.

To me, it is not a worthwhile question to debate the existence or nonexistence of God. One way or the other, the spiritual realm is beyond the power of the human mind to describe, and as soon as we attempt to put our experience of it into words, we have already shrunken it, regardless of how beautifully we speak. If it is helpful for you to conceive of God as a specific entity, then by all means, do so. There is indeed great truth to be found in many descriptions of God, but I would implore you not to let these descriptions confine your perception of possibility. Rather, allow them to simply be a starting point.

Brain Wave Vibration is one among many training methods I have developed to help people stop thinking about spirituality so that they can start experiencing it.

Seeking Oneness

When you consider the many different manifestations of spiritual experience in the world, it obviously does no good to debate which one is right. That has been the root of unbelievable amounts of suffering in the world. In fact, in the way I see spirituality, it is quite contradictory to differentiate in this way. It is best rather to focus on the concepts we have in common.

Most spiritual traditions have at their root the notion of the ultimate peace that comes through the oneness of all beings. The Bible speaks of "the peace that surpasses all understanding," and Hindus speak of nirvana. My belief is that journeying to this place of oneness is the only thing that ultimately matters in any spiritual practice.

Much of our mythology teaches us that life is about finding our way back to oneness. In Korean traditions, we have the story of Mago, an Earth spirit analogous to Mother Earth in Western society. At one point, humanity was in accord with Mago, and there was a state of perfect peace and harmony. As in the biblical story of Eden, this paradise was eventually lost as people began to divide themselves.

According to the mythologies of many cultures, humanity once lived harmoniously, only to lose this perfect existence. The story of Adam and Eve in the Garden of Eden is a familiar example. I believe these stories are a reflection of the paradise that already lies within the human brain. I am certain that we have the potential for perfect joy and harmony already written into the structure of our brain. So what then is it that keeps us from living accordingly?

In the Eden story, the first man and woman ate of the fruit of the Tree of Knowledge of Good and Evil. It is significant that knowledge and judgment of right and wrong—ideas created and processed in the prefrontal cortex—were responsible for the downfall of humankind. As soon as we began separating good from evil, we began separating ourselves from one another and the rest of the universe.

While this may seem regrettable, it is also fortunate on many levels. Differentiation separates, but it also provides the chance for reunification. Separation gives us a chance to truly value the experience of oneness, in much the same way that both light and shadow are needed to create the perception of form. If we had simply kept our oneness from the beginning of time, there would have been no chance to choose oneness through our own free will, which is the choice we have to make now.

Experiencing Oneness

The question then is how to return to this place of oneness. I believe that it is through quieting the mind and the experience of energy that we can return.

Brain Wave Vibration can open the door to this possibility because it offers a way to stop the thinking mind, even if only for a few minutes. When you practice well, you will feel a disintegration of the surface of your body. Of course, it is not a literal disintegration—your skin and the rest of your body will remain intact. What you will realize, however, is that you do not end there, that your being goes far beyond the confines of your body. You will experience that directly, not just as an intellectual concept.

I once had a student who was a Buddhist nun. Like most monks, she spent many hours a day meditating, looking for that very state of oneness. She was very distracted, however, because she found that her health began to deteriorate. She could not sleep or sit still for long because of serious kidney problems. She began to practice Brain Wave Vibration and had immediate improvements in her health, and was finally able to focus properly for meditation. She says she now knows what Buddha meant when he said, "Find truth in your body; outside you will not find it in a thousand years."

It is very important to pay attention to the experience of energy in your body as you practice Brain Wave Vibration. Energy is the real stuff of life, and it is through energy that oneness reveals itself. If you can quiet your mind sufficiently, you will sense this in your body as a subtle but consistent vibration.

If you allow this sensation to expand, you will not sense any end to this energy and you will glimpse the infinite nature of the universe. This greater cosmic energy I call *Chun-ji-ki-un*, which literally translates as "the circulation of heaven and earth energy." To connect to this energy is to connect to the ultimate energy pulsing through all of existence—what some may call the Source and others call God.

There is a part of your brain that exists to connect to this energy. You can conceptualize it as a radio receiver picking up invisible messages from the cosmos. When your brain waves are agitated, it is like static interrupting the signal. Please use Brain Wave Vibration as a way to clear out the static and tune in to the greater peace and serenity of the cosmos.

Highway to the Higher Self

Have you ever stopped to think about why people all over the world have some concept of God or some higher intelligence at the center of existence? Some people, especially those who would like to dismiss the notion of God from modern life, claim that God is merely a fanciful illusion born out of the human inability to come to terms with mortality and other difficult problems of human existence. Certainly it may be true that some of the incarnations of deities in various cultures are effected by aspects of human psychology, but I think that is not the entire story.

I think that God exists in the human psyche as a kind of beacon that beckons humanity toward a higher state of existence. In this sense, it does not really matter whether God exists or does not exist in the conventional sense. God does exist because God exists in the human mind. Various cultures have various versions of God that reflect a people's needs and values at a particular point in history. In my opinion, even if you are an atheist or agnostic, God exists within you just the same, in the form of all your highest ideals and dreams. The conceptions of God that lead to hatred and bloodshed are not God at all, but rather they are tragically skewed and egotistical attempts to define and limit that which is ineffable and boundless by its very nature.

When we tap into the greatness within us, we are tapping into the God within us. This is the essence of what we call miracles. Miracles, I believe, do not come from someplace supernatural, but rather from a place that is both deep inside us and yet so vast as to be beyond the small thing we usually call self.

The story of one man I know illustrates the real meaning of miracles. On my journey, I have met many people who have multiple physical and spiritual problems, but this man's suffering was extraordinary. From infancy onward, he was plagued by a parade of maladies. Born with an undescended testicle that was removed at age five, he developed testicular cancer in the remaining organ as a young adult. Given a blood transfusion during one of his treatments, he then contracted hepatitis C, which badly affected his liver. Eventually he required surgery on his liver, which sadly resulted in damage to his spine, leaving him paraplegic, paralyzed from the middle of the chest downward.

From there, his health condition plummeted even further. He had four strokes and developed diabetes, hypertension, and immune problems. He was at the end of his rope. Brain Wave Vibration seemed like his last hope, and the fact that he could participate fully, even in his wheelchair, appealed to him greatly, so he gave it a try.

This man discovered that when he practiced Brain Wave Vibration, he felt as though the vibrations extended throughout his body, in spite of the fact that he had no literal sensation in his lower body. Remarkably, he recovered the use of a portion of his spine, known as the 4T section, and his blood pressure, glucose level, and liver function all returned to normal within a few months. He and his doctors were amazed.

What accounts for such miraculous healing? The man now says, in spite of his physical problems, "I found that the brain controls it all, and it is still working just fine in spite of everything else." He unleashed his brain's power by first allowing it to feel hope, something the medical establishment, for all its advanced treatments, was unable to provide to him. In addition, he soon turned his mind to helping others, as he decided to help wheelchair-bound veterans learn the same techniques.

This turning outward toward others is, I believe, an important part of anyone's recovery. It helps us overcome the root cause of most problems we face, both physical and spiritual. The process begins with hope and then radiates out from us to those we love. By connecting to others, we also connect to ourselves, overcoming our separation to find the deeper, infinite meaning of wholeness.

CHAPTER 8

The Power of Hope

*I believe in humanity. We are an incredible species. We're still just a
child creature, and we're still being nasty to each other. All children go
through these phases. We're growing up; we're moving into adolescence
now. When we grow up——man, we're going to be something!*

—Gene Roddenberry, creator of *Star Trek*

IT IS EASY TO GET DISCOURAGED in
today's world. There are many human problems that dominate
our headlines and preoccupy our minds. It can seem like the
world is getting increasingly worse. There is no doubt that we
need to change our ways or risk serious consequences.

I think, however, that all our troubles can turn around in an
instant. All of the negativity we face is just a manifestation of our
inner world, and just as a mood or a thought can change instantly, so can the world.

The important point is to look not at the temporary state
of the world but at what is under the surface. If you believe that
people truly desire peace, then there is no reason to despair. If

people act selfishly, it is only because they have been momentarily blinded by their current situation. Give up your need to judge or cast blame on others, regardless of how rotten their behavior may seem. The most effective action you can take is to act on your own true nature, and soon others will do the same when they are ready. Go beyond the world of thought, put your true nature into action, and the rest of the world will follow.

You need only one thing in the world. It is not money. It is not fame. It is not even food. All you need in the world is hope. As long as you have that, you have everything. This is your birthright that you should never lose. If you keep hope, all your other necessities will come soon enough.

You Are the Earth

I suggest that we all seek reconnection to the Earth as a source of hope in the world. First of all, the Earth is our one common value, and it can be the means of reuniting humanity. No matter how different you look or how strange your culture may seem to me, we both rely completely on this Earth. As seen from space, the Earth has no real borders, except where the planet ends and space begins. We must rally around the Earth soon, or we risk losing her along with our own survival. We need to realize that she, the Earth, is our one common bond and the source of our only true identity.

We speak sometimes of being Americans or Koreans or Brazilians or Africans, but in reality, all we really are is Earth citizens. Nationalistic identities and borders are nothing more than illusions of separation. Imagine how this simple shift in consciousness could transform our environmental and political outlook for the better.

The Hopi, the native people who inhabit land near my home in Sedona, Arizona, apply a system of energetic physiology to the Earth that closely parallels the physiology of the human being. According to their tradition, the Earth turns on an axis, which functions like the human backbone. Along this backbone can be found a series of energy centers, analogous to the chakras in the human body, which resonate a primal musical tone in harmony with all creation. Humanity, as they see it, is just a microcosm of the Earth. We have been given the gift of musical, verbal, and artistic expression not for our own glory but as a means of giving expression to the Earth and all creation (Kalweit).

I would like to propose that direct, positive experience of and interaction with nature is essential to your health. Since the dawn of the Industrial Revolution, humankind has become increasingly disconnected from the Earth that sustains us, and the effect has been regrettable. In the most obvious ways, human health is currently threatened by environmental problems, such as pollution and greenhouse gases. But I would also like to suggest that the effects of this go deeper, that disconnection from nature is essentially a spiritual problem that subsequently leads to problems of the body and mind as well.

Author Richard Louv, in his book *Last Child in the Woods: Saving Our Children from Nature-Deficit Disorder*, suggests that many of the mental and emotional problems that have become increasingly prevalent in children are linked to their decreasing amount of direct contact with nature. He cites one study in which kids with attention deficit/hyperactivity disorder (ADHD) were found to focus better on tasks when in natural settings instead of urban surroundings.

If you find yourself unable to concentrate, perhaps you will agree that not only children can fall victim to nature-deficit disorder. I would contend that part of the reason adults are increasingly stricken with anxiety, depression, and other forms of psychological distress is because they are simply not grounded.

I mean *grounded* here in the most literal sense: people are disconnected from the very Earth that sustains their lives. It is evident in the ways we produce our food, choose to work, and interact with one another. As we disconnect from nature, we also seem to disconnect from each other; our relationships sour and our mental health is compromised. And, as we continue to ignore the important role of the Earth in our lives, we allow the planet to slip ever closer to environmental ruin, and we unintentionally invite the myriad physical illnesses that accompany this—cancer, respiratory disorders, endocrine disruption, and so forth.

Develop a Wide-Benefit Brain

The best thing you can do to bring a sense of hope to your life is to discover a sense of purpose. But how can you know your real purpose? Maybe you have searched for that for thirty or forty years and have never found the answer.

I cannot answer that question exactly for you because it is ultimately up to you. What I do know is that whatever mission you choose in life, you will undoubtedly be of great service to humanity. I believe that every person has a great internal desire to find a harmonious way of living on the planet and to contribute something of value to the world. In Korean, we call this the *hong-ik* ideal, which refers to the desire to be beneficial, not just to yourself and your kin, but to all humanity.

This sort of mind-set can be a great source of continual hope in your life. People who have a clear sense of purpose are never hopeless because they always know they can make a difference, even if just one step at a time.

There is a natural progression to life that unfortunately many of us have stepped away from. It is as if many of us are caterpillars who have decided not to become butterflies. Or maybe we have just forgotten that we are able to become butterflies.

As I see it, the human life span has three phases. First, we have a growth phase that usually is experienced during childhood, adolescence, and our early twenties. Of course we continue to grow throughout our lives, but this time of life is for most of us a particularly intense period of investigation and experimentation during which we try to get to know ourselves and the world.

In our late twenties and thirties, we move into what I call the "success phase," during which we try to create something tangible with our lives in the physical world, perhaps through career or the development of our finances. The problem is that most people seem to get stuck in this success phase, thinking it is the most important aspect of life. This is a little like a caterpillar thinking he can do no more with his life than spend it eating leaves all day.

In reality, the caterpillar has the ability to transform into a beautiful butterfly, just as you can transform far beyond success in the physical world. Not realizing this, many people choose material success only to feel unfulfilled when it finally arrives.

These perpetual caterpillars do not understand that there is one more stage, the most important stage, that is the source of true and lasting happiness. This is the stage I call "completion of the soul." Once you have accomplished success in the "real" world, however you choose to define that, you can achieve the butterfly stage by turning your mind toward a different kind of success in which you find full expression of your highest sense of self. This can begin at any age, but older adulthood is the ideal time, a time when many other longings have been fulfilled.

Completion means reaching a state of full awakening, in which you feel and live according to a continuous state of oneness. This means stepping beyond the ego of the small self to fulfill your mission of service to humanity. At this point your mind will be enveloped in constant joy, and you will be finally able to become that beautiful, fluttering butterfly.

Vibratory Resonance

In many ways, our senses fool us into thinking that various people and objects in the world are separate from each other. Now physics tells us that there are no distinct boundaries between anything or anyone.

In a very practical way, you can see how vibrations can influence us. You have certainly experienced walking into a room that feels heavy and negative. Sometimes this may be because the people in the room have just been arguing or discussing a somber topic. Even if they have stopped talking, or even if they have left the room, you can still feel it. This is the effect of those people's brain waves on the surrounding atmosphere.

Even inanimate objects can carry vibrations that influence us. Sometimes a room feels negative, not because of some human event but because of the vibration inherent in the objects in the room. You could say that interior decorators and artists are masters of vibration, manipulating the way colors and shapes interact to affect the human brain.

The experience of beauty is the experience of vibrations that resonate with you in a way that opens you up to the world around you. If you have ever experienced the feeling of awe, you have experienced the feeling of expansion that can come through beauty. When this happens, your brain is recognizing the high-level vibrations it craves. This sense of beauty can come in the form of beautiful objects, people, or actions. And the really wonderful truth is this: as you expand your brain's ability, more and more of the world's beauty will become apparent to you, until finally the whole beautiful picture of reality is revealed to you.

If the color and shape of objects can have so much influence on us, imagine how much influence we can have on each other. I am sure you have experienced that when someone is in a bad mood, that mood tends to rub off on you. By the same token, someone's smile can completely turn your day around. Imagine what a difference we could make if we really tried to put this to full use. Enough people producing positive brain waves could change the world, don't you think?

A change in collective human consciousness essentially requires an invisible and inaudible communication between brains. As you learn to orient your brain toward positive information, the whole of humanity will be lifted up as well. That may seem overwhelming at first, but it requires only that you first change your own brain to work in a way that is most healthy for your own body and the Earth.

I view your brain stem as a marvelous antenna that can send and receive messages to and from the world around you. This medium of communication is called *Chun-ji-ki-un*, or cosmic energy. Because you are connected to all other living beings through this cosmic energy, you are an integral player in creating a better, more sustainable way of life on this planet.

No one has to teach you to dislike negative energy waves. It is a wisdom already written into your brain. Complex arguments about morality will seem moot if we just learn to respond to energy rather than to each other's words. Take a look at this list of human attributes:

- Happiness
- Despair
- Honesty
- Loyalty
- Sadness
- Love
- Hope
- Disdain
- Brutality
- Gratitude

I'm sure you could label each one "negative" or "positive" without a second thought. It does not require analysis, and no one has to work hard to convince you that one is better than the other. This is because some of these traits are indicative of people with positive brain waves, while others carry a more negative vibration. No one has to debate about the rightness or wrongness of these traits because your brain knows instinctively which ones promote health and which detract. Essentially, your brain craves positive vibrations that help keep it healthy, just as your body craves the nutrients that promote health.

Developing Infinite Mind

You may wonder why humanity so often chooses negative consciousness vibrations when the brain's natural inclination is to choose positive ones. In fact, when you look at the events of history and the current state of the world, you might be inclined to think that we choose negatively more often than not.

Basically, humanity has become addicted to negative information. At some point in our development, perhaps through overdependence on our rational minds, we convinced ourselves that life is all about competition and acquisition. We concocted myths about the scarcity of goods, and we invented the need to judge ourselves superior to our neighbors. Worst of all, we decided that power is something that comes from outside ourselves. Thus we began fighting to ensure our place in a world of perceived limitations.

Even though we appear to be fighting for our own gain, the negativity has turned inward as well, blocking us from the true source of empowerment that exists within us. Negativity of all sorts has become a substitute for real power because real empowerment is rarely considered. Children too often grow up thinking nationality, grades, popularity, and the like make them who they are.

It is no wonder, then, that so many young people feel burdened by a sense of disillusionment as they reach adulthood. Teenagers, especially those who have grown up in very disempowering environments, demonstrate this in their self-destructive behaviors and attitudes. Feeling powerless, they turn to negative behaviors and thinking patterns as a substitute for real power. Youth should be a time of joyous self-discovery and development, but for too many young people, adolescence becomes a time of self-loathing and aimless wandering.

This is why I believe we need a drastic educational revolution. We need reform of a whole new kind—not the kind that has to do with test scores and grades but the kind of educational reform that will empower children to find their own happiness. The current system of competition and evaluation is unnecessarily disempowering, even for the few who excel within the system. This is why I developed Brain Education.

The objective of Brain Education is to give people the ability to use their brain operating system effectively. We get an owner's manual when we buy a car, a computer, or any other technological gadget, but unfortunately we do not get an owner's manual for our most complex technology—the brain. It would be great if we received one when we were born, wouldn't it? It would be great if we could just look in a book to find out how to manage our emotions, how to maximize our abilities, and how to find peace in a hectic world.

In a way, though, we do have this owner's manual, but we must relearn how to read it. It exists in the form of the inherent wisdom that is every person's birthright. If we can just get out of its way, all of this wisdom is right there, written into the very nature of the brain itself.

I know that if you are reading this book you are already interested in your own self-development. That is rare and wonderful in itself, but I would like you to make one small shift in your perspective on that. Please change your self-development mind into your infinite-development mind. In other words, really believe in your true potential and feel the joy of your own infinite nature. Run, do not walk, forward—the world is waiting for you. Don't settle for good enough; stop making limits. To create limits is to deny life, and limits are a desecration of your brain.

The Return to Oneness

I believe that everything in human existence is part of the great unfolding of consciousness in the universe. All the saints and sages of the world have been giving essentially the same message that contains a plea to return to oneness. Even the sciences have moved us in that direction. For example, Einstein's search for a unified field theory, his elusive "theory of everything," can be seen as this same yearning for oneness in scientific form. It is a defining characteristic that science separates and labels, hence the classification system into which living things are divided—phylum, class, order, and so forth. But quantum physics, as represented in books like *The Tao of Physics* and in films like *What the Bleep Do We Know!?*, shows that when we divide things into smaller and smaller particles, everything is just energy. We eventually come back to the same conclusion as the ancient sages did long ago—form is illusion and all are one.

I believe that information comes to us in three important forms, and together these elements have amazing power to transform brain waves—as well as lives and ultimately our entire planet.

First, there is *music*, which contains the power to create mood and evoke emotion. Second, there is *message*, which forms the structure of our belief systems and influences the quality of our relationships. Third, there is *action*, which is the ultimate reflection of our brains' content.

If we can learn to use all three of these things well, I think we can find great hope for ourselves and the planet. A favorite song of mine—"From a Distance," sung by Bette Midler and composed by Julie Gold—has two of these three elements. It combines music with message for a powerful effect—and it can also inspire you to act if you believe in its message. I love the lyrics, because they remind me where we are all going:

From a distance the world looks blue and green,
and the snow-capped mountains white.

From a distance the ocean meets the stream,
and the eagle takes to flight.

From a distance, there is harmony,
and it echoes through the land.
It's the voice of hope, it's the voice of peace,
it's the voice of every man.

From a distance we all have enough,
and no one is in need.
And there are no guns, no bombs, and no disease,
no hungry mouths to feed.

From a distance we are instruments
marching in a common band.
Playing songs of hope, playing songs of peace.
They're the songs of every man.

God is watching us. God is watching us.
God is watching us from a distance.

From a distance you look like my friend,
even though we are at war.
From a distance I just cannot comprehend
what all this fighting is for.

From a distance there is harmony,

and it echoes through the land.
And it's the hope of hopes, it's the love of loves,
it's the heart of every man.
It's the hope of hopes, it's the love of loves.
This is the song of every man.

And God is watching us, God is watching us,
God is watching us from a distance.
Oh, God is watching us, God is watching.
God is watching us from a distance.

This song sums up all we need to transform our lives and the world—and it encompasses the highest purpose of Brain Wave Vibration. I hope that Brain Wave Vibration can give you the distance you need to see your own life, and all the problems that come with human existence, from a distance—even if only for a few moments at a time. As you step away from your constant thinking and continual worries, I think you will be able to see the blessings that lie in everything. From that place you will begin to see the beautiful perfection of it all and will come closer to the perfection that already lies within you.

This is a beautiful and hopeful time to be alive. We are at a turning point, and your contribution to the world is needed more than ever. All of your struggles, all the struggles of your ancestors, all the struggles of all life have led to this moment right now. You are the culmination of life's great yearning; you are the hope of the world.

PART II

Practice

THE JOURNEY BEGINS

An ounce of action is worth a ton of theory.
—Ralph Waldo Emerson, philosopher

NOW YOU HAVE ARRIVED at the most important part of Brain Wave Vibration—the actual practice of the method. The principles behind it are important, and I hope you will keep them in mind for continued inspiration and guidance. But they are all of no use unless you put these principles into deliberate, intentional practice.

The mind-set you keep during this practice is very important. Please approach it with an emphatic sense of intention. Plan on using this as a tool by which you will transform yourself, not just as a physical fitness routine. Believe fully that a perfected version of you waits just below the surface of your existence, and use this method as a way to shake off all the false layers of misidentification that have been standing in your way.

As you practice, hold in your mind a picture of the person you want to be. Visualize the picture in full color with every minuscule detail in place. At first this image of your perfected self may not be very clear to you. You may be undecided as to who you really want to be. If this is the case, don't worry. It is natural at the beginning of any journey. You don't know what the Grand Canyon is like until you go there, right? But you can imagine it, and that imagination is an important part of what will propel you toward it.

Just focus intently, and soon you will become clearer and clearer to yourself. You can start with a general idea of who you want to be by setting small, attainable goals. As you gain confidence and awareness, your true identity will become increasingly obvious, like an image emerging on a Polaroid photograph.

Most importantly, always remember that this training is for you. You are not doing it to please anyone or to gain anything from someone else. This is a precious moment with yourself in a world that is always calling you outside yourself. Even five minutes of practice can become eternal if you allow yourself to go deep inside to explore the infinite landscape within you.

I wish you great joy and peace as you embark on your journey of discovery.

GUIDELINES FOR PRACTICE

T HERE ARE FEW RULES for Brain Wave Vibration. You will be surprised to discover that with practice you can experience the benefits of the method almost anywhere and in a variety of forms. Although I am offering you some guidelines to get started, Brain Wave Vibration is an exercise that is continually reinventing itself. Ultimately, there may be as many forms as there are practitioners. As you discover more about your body and its response to vibration, you will likely adjust your practice to suit your particular needs. There are no hard-and-fast rules about the practice of Brain Wave Vibration. But in the meantime, here are some basic guidelines that will help you get off to a good start:

Bigger isn't always better.

When people first start practicing Brain Wave Vibration, they sometimes think that making bigger and faster movements will result in better effects, but this is not necessarily so. They are used to thinking that the harder they work at a something, the better the results will be. This is often true, but you must re-member that Brain Wave Vibration works on a very different principle than other exercise forms. Brain Wave Vibration is not about moving the muscles, pumping the heart, or burning calo-ries, although all these things may offer added benefits. Rather, it is about improving the energy system of the body, especially as it relates to your brain. This could mean that very subtle vi-brations are all that are needed. In fact, large, flamboyant move-ments will tend to draw you into the outside world, which is not the desired effect. As you begin, focus on your body to discover your own natural rhythm. Begin with simple, subtle movement and let the sensation grow from there.

Practice anytime, for as long as feels appropriate.

Many people say that they cannot stick to their fitness routines because they simply don't have time. With Brain Wave Vibration, you don't get to use that excuse. There is no specific amount of time needed to practice it. A session could last from 3 minutes to an hour or more. Any break during the day—even while sitting at your desk—can be turned into a Brain Wave Vibration break. The results you get depend on how well you focus and how deep you are willing to go into the vibrations, not on the amount of time you spend doing it. Start with several 3- to 5-minute ses-sions, then gradually increase the amount of time you spend on a single session. Eventually work up to sessions of 10 minutes or more to recharge the body with fresh energy. Later, you will learn to consciously adjust the strength of the vibration and the amount of time spent to suit the condition of your body.

Consider your environment.

You can practice Brain Wave Vibration just about anywhere, but you will find that different locations provide different effects. You can easily practice right at your desk with simple versions of Brain Wave Vibration, such as the Head Nod (page 183), even in the middle of a busy office. However, sometimes you may wish to go more deeply into the vibration than that sort of environment will allow. In that case, it is ideal to practice in a quiet place with few distractions where no one will interrupt. If you have a chance to do so, it is also a good idea to practice with others at a training center. When practicing with others, a resonance of the brain waves occurs that deepens the experience and enhances the effect.

Be confident.

This method is so simple that it can be mastered just by reading this book. However, when trying it for the first time, it is natural to feel awkward about the process and to wonder if your posture is correct. You may worry about looking silly, or you may have some doubts about the method's validity. Try to empty your mind of these thoughts and just follow the natural wisdom of your body. Remember that there is no right or wrong way to practice. If you are sincere and are willing to focus on yourself, your results will be excellent.

Choose your music well.

Strictly speaking, Brain Wave Vibration practice does not require music. It is about your own internal rhythms, not about moving to a beat as you would when you dance. However, music can be helpful when you begin. Obviously, very slow and sentimental music is not suitable for the vibration. The most effective music for Brain Wave Vibration is music with a strong basic beat, such as that found in many forms of traditional drumming. I find Korean *sa-mul-no-ri* to be especially effective because it awakens the brain with a lively combination of sounds from gongs and drums, generating a powerful vibration that you can feel throughout your body. In addition to sa-mul-no-ri, percussive folk instruments from Africa and South America offer a simple, primitive repetition of sound that replicates the basic rhythms of life. Music is helpful to induce the proper state of mind for Brain Wave Vibration in the beginning, but as time goes by, the rhythm of the body should overpower the rhythm of the music. Be sure to focus inward at all times and allow your own rhythm to come forward.

Send a positive message to yourself.

The goal of Brain Wave Vibration is to completely quiet the mind so that the latent powers of the brain can come to the forefront. However, this is not so easy for most people, since they are accustomed to constant, habitual chatter in their minds. Instead of vainly trying to shut off your mind, you can concentrate on a single positive thought. Choose something highly empowering that relates to your personal vision. For example, it could be something as simple as, "I am whole. I am one." Chant this to yourself, either silently or aloud, as a personal mantra while you practice. Through this process, the vibrations of your own voice will add to the overall effect on your brain waves and will strengthen your transformational intent. If you have any weakness, pain, or disease in your body, you can also say the name of that particular body part as you practice Brain Wave Vibration. For example, if you are having a problem with your heart, then repeat a simple, affirmative statement, such as "Healthy heart, healthy heart."

Breathe well.

Because of our rushed, stressful way of life, most of us do not breathe properly. Our breath becomes shallow and unstable. Do not force your breath, but focus on breathing naturally while you are practicing Brain Wave Vibration. Focus on exhaling completely because this will help you release tension from the body.

Also, open your mouth a little bit to allow your breath to flow freely. Imagine that you are expelling all the negative energy from your body through your mouth and nose.

Expect ups and downs.

In Dahn Yoga there is a phrase, *Myung-hyun*, which refers to an energetic phenomenon that occurs as the body changes. Myung-hyun literally means "the intersection of light and dark," and it reflects the fact that negative energy will be expelled as fresh, new energy comes into the body. Some people experience this transformation in the form of body aches as if they have a cold or fatigue and heaviness in the body. However, it can take many forms, both physical and psychological. Myung-hyun occurs when the once-blocked ki flow is restored, which can be uncomfortable. It is actually a good sign and should not discourage you from further practice. In fact, the more you practice, the quicker the symptoms will subside. It is a sign that your energetic condition is improving. The symptoms should be mild and temporary, so seek a doctor's advice if you have any serious or long-lasting symptoms.

PRECAUTIONS FOR PRACTICE

BRAIN WAVE VIBRATION IS SO SIMPLE that it can be done by anyone of any age in just about any condition. However, like any exercise, you should not push yourself beyond your limits, and you should discuss your plans with your physician if you are concerned at all about your physical readiness to participate. Here are some precautions to keep in mind:

If you are older or very weak…

You first need to stimulate your physical energy. The center of that energy is located in your lower abdomen, about two inches below your navel. Before beginning the Full-Body Brain Wave Vibration exercise, warm up with the Abdominal Vibration exercise on page 190. When you begin full-body practice, start with only very slight vibratory movements. If you stand during practice, make sure your feet are planted solidly on the ground and that your knees are slightly bent. If necessary, assume a seated or lying posture. You can also practice while balancing against a stable object, such as a wall or a sturdy piece of furniture.

If you become dizzy easily...

It is probably because your energy tends to gather in your head. If your energy then suddenly drops toward your lower body, you may feel dizzy. Since most people today have too much energy in the head, dizziness is a fairly common occurrence as the energy system begins to return to a healthy state. The key to overcoming this problem is to learn to center your energy in your lower abdomen (called *Dahn-jon*) through relaxed concentration. Before you begin regular Brain Wave Vibration training, practice Abdominal Vibration (page 172) for several minutes. Relax your shoulders completely and visualize energy settling in the lower abdomen. Continue until the abdomen feels warm. After Abdominal Vibration, breathe deeply in and out three times, releasing all remaining tension from the body. Close your eyes and feel the vibrations circulating through the body. Dizziness can also occur if you stop Brain Wave Vibration training too suddenly, so make sure you ease to a stop after practice.

If you are extremely tense...

Work up to the exercise. Most people carry a lot of excess tension in their bodies. Sometimes the same patterns of tension have been repeated for years, so it can be hard to let go of the tension. Basically, this is your body's habit, which is the direct result of your brain's habits. If you attempt to perform Brain

Wave Vibration in this state, you could pull a muscle or cause some other injury in the body. Besides that, you will have a hard time feeling the vibrations in your body if circulation is blocked by tension. Before starting Brain Wave Vibration practice, relax your body by slowly turning your head left and right and rotating the shoulders forward and back. You can also do a few stretching exercises before you begin. As you start Brain Wave Vibration, make small, gentle movements and build up to more dramatic ones.

If you cannot breathe well because of asthma or cardiovascular problems...

As you exhale, make a long "ahhh" sound while patting the chest to open up the airway. Focus on exhaling all air out of the lungs. You will feel a subtle vibration that spreads out from the chest to the whole body. Chest Twist Vibration (page 188) will be especially helpful to you.

If you are experiencing or recovering from an extended illness...

You can still practice Brain Wave Vibration, but you should take steps to conserve your energy during practice. You can easily practice from a lying position, and you can do it with the help of a caregiver. Lie down comfortably, relax your body, and close your eyes. The caregiver should hold both of your feet and lift up your legs slightly. The caregiver can then begin to shake the feet and bounce the legs gently up and down. You will feel the vibration starting from the feet and spreading to the whole body. Lying in bed for a long time can stagnate the energy circulation of the body, so practicing a mild vibration of this sort can make the body feel refreshed and lighter.

If you have arthritis or other joint problems...

Pain in your joints may become distracting or discourage you from practice. To combat this, start with very slight movements in the joints to bring increased circulation to these parts. Also, if you do feel pain, concentrate on exhaling the pain along with the breath. Visualize healing energy from the brain stem traveling through the body to the joints. As the pain decreases, increase your vibration to envelop the entire body.

THE PROCESS OF BRAIN WAVE VIBRATION

Brain Wave Vibration is so simple there is no need to analyze the method too closely. However, for the sake of understanding, you should be aware that there are three distinct phases of the training. In actual practice, these steps should happen automatically without any clear distinction between each phase. It may take a few repetitions, a proper environment, and some extra time to fully experience all three phases.

....

Step 1: Deliberately make vibrations in your body.

....

When you begin, you will make the vibrations consciously. You may do so by following the beat of a song, or you may just follow a rhythm that seems appropriate to you. At this stage you should focus on relaxing the body as you move to the rhythm. Try to quiet the thinking mind by focusing only on the beat and the movement of your body. Avoid self-conscious concern about how you look to others; just focus on yourself. To begin, gently shake the head left and right. As the neck starts feeling relaxed, shake the shoulders up and down. Let the sensation spread through your body as you shake your entire body while lightly bouncing up and down. As you shake, imagine that you are shaking off all your complicated thoughts and emotions. Try to release all tension from the body through your exhalation.

Step 2: Let the entire body ride the rhythm.

Once your body is fully relaxed and your mind has quieted, you can begin to follow the natural rhythm. Focus intently on your physical sensations. Allow the vibration to spread out to all parts of your body. As the body starts riding the rhythm, it becomes completely relaxed, and the skin starts vibrating. The breathing becomes natural, and all the motions follow their own rhythm. At this time you will begin to make spontaneous movement with your body. This is the process of the body healing itself. Small, subtle vibrations become bigger as they start getting more deeply into the rhythm.

Step 3: Follow the flow of energy.

Once the vibration becomes natural and familiar, you will become increasingly aware of the movement of energy within your body. Allow yourself to follow that flow. Just like hitting the accelerator in order to speed up a vehicle, this increased energy will speed up and strengthen the waves of the vibration in your body. While the movements tend to get bigger at this point, they will also become more graceful and free-flowing. Your body's natural healing instincts will take over at this point, and you will find that you automatically assume unique postures that promote healing for your particular bodily condition.

SEVEN GOALS OF BRAIN WAVE VIBRATION

1. Maintain healthier brain waves.

Studies have shown that there is great benefit in learning how to lower your brain waves from the highly alert beta waves to the more relaxed alpha or theta waves. Traditionally, this has been achieved through biofeedback or meditation. However, biofeedback requires expensive equipment, and meditation requires highly focused training. In Brain Wave Vibration, on the other hand, lowered brain waves can be accomplished extraordinarily easily. Through simple repetition and movement, the brain waves are instantly calmed and stabilized.

2. Manage your stress.

During Brain Wave Vibration, you will experience a deep sense of relaxation. This is a very important benefit, since most of us are in a continual state of stress. Constant stress is hugely debilitating for the body, and many physical and psychological diseases can eventually result. During practice, your parasympathetic nervous system is given a chance to bring your body back to a state of healthy equilibrium.

3. Activate all parts of the brain.

Just by moving your body, you will activate your brain in ways that sedentary behaviors, no matter how mentally rigorous, cannot. Why? Because all parts of your body are connected to your brain, and when you move, many diverse parts of your brain are stimulated simultaneously. And beyond that, Brain Wave Vibration helps shift mental emphasis away from the thinking part of the brain, the prefrontal cortex, so that all parts of the brain can begin to function in beneficial ways. In particular, the brain stem can start to create balance in the body in ways that might otherwise be undermined by the stress-producing thoughts of the prefrontal cortex. Also, negative emotional content can finally be released and replaced with positive information. The rhythmic vibrations and spontaneous movements can also help activate creativity and imagination as you are transported to a place beyond the rational mind.

4. Develop positive habits.

Your brain has an amazing ability to restructure itself according to your wishes. However, your brain's neural connections can also become rigid through repeated patterns of behavior, and thus it can be very hard to change negative habits once they are solidified in your brain. Brain Wave Vibration helps you achieve a relaxed, open state of mind that will better facilitate the development of new mental and physical habits.

5. Create happiness.

Many people carry around a lot of emotional baggage that prevents them from fully experiencing the joy of life. On top of that, they have a lot of preconceptions and judgments that prevent them from simply being present in the moment and enjoying the beauty of the world as it exists. The primary goal of Brain Wave Vibration is to help you return to a simple state of being, a place where you can experience yourself and the world without thought or judgment. With practice, it will become natural to discard old, debilitating emotions and to develop a positive state of mind.

6. Restore a healthy energy condition in your body.

In Asian medical systems, health of the body is dependent on the flow of life energy through the body. This energy, called *ki* or *chi*, runs through channels in the body called meridians. If these meridians are blocked, pain or disease result. Muscle tension is a common source of energy blockage. Brain Wave Vibration helps release tension that blocks the flow of ki energy in the body, thereby improving your overall sense of vitality and health.

7. Expand your awareness of yourself and the universe.

Ultimately, this training method is for your growth as a person. This means to go deeply within yourself and, as a result, to expand beyond yourself to something much larger than your ego's limited sense of self. Brain Wave Vibration, by quieting the thinking mind, allows you, at least for a few moments, to tap into the greater rhythm and flow of the universe as a whole.

BASIC BRAIN WAVE VIBRATION

ULTIMATELY, YOU CAN DO the training in any number of different postures, and you can create your own postures as you learn to follow the flow of energy and the needs of your body. You can do the training with or without music, but you may find that music with a strong basic rhythm will help you get into the natural rhythms of your own body more quickly. The most important point is to just enjoy yourself and to let your thinking mind drift away.

These postures are the most basic forms of Brain Wave Vibration, and I recommend that you follow them in the beginning. After that, you can start improvising according to the dictates of your bodily needs. Immediately following this chapter you will find some variations that many students have found particularly useful.

The Head Nod Method

This is one of the most simple and convenient forms of Brain Wave Vibration. It can be done anytime during the day to refresh your brain, even sitting at a desk while working or studying. You can also try this while lying down before sleeping. The Head Nod Method is designed to deliver vibrations directly to the brain stem for deep relaxation and release of tension. After this exercise, you will be able to focus and retain information more successfully. It will also help you avoid the stiff neck and shoulders that often accompany work and study. Try it for just three minutes in the afternoons when you feel fatigued, and you will feel much more energized.

1. Sit in a chair with your arms resting comfortably at your sides or in front of you on a desk. You may also sit on the floor in a half-lotus posture. When sitting in a chair, do not lean your back against the chair, but keep your back straight.
2. Close your eyes and breathe comfortably, relaxing your body completely.
3. Begin gently shaking your head from side to side. It is normal to hear some noise from the neck as you begin, but this will lessen with practice. Breathe fully, focusing especially on the exhalation.

4. Focus on your brain stem, located at the point where your head pivots left and right.

5. Visualize your brain stem and entire brain lighting up as you go deeper and deeper into the shaking motion. Your head may also go up and down or follow the shape of an infinity symbol as you go deeper into the motion.

6. After a few minutes, slowly return to external awareness, breathing in and exhaling fully.

Full-Body Brain Wave Vibration

The goal with the Full-Body Brain Wave Vibration is to create full relaxation and a calm, meditative mental state. With practice you will be able to bring yourself more deeply into the vibrations, and the benefits will become greater. You can eventually grow the vibrations to include the whole body, changing the posture as seems intuitively appropriate to you. There is no specific time requirement for Brain Wave Vibration, but you might want to start this exercise with 10 minutes and work up to 20 to 30 minutes.

As you become more comfortable with this exercise, work on letting go of your inhibitions. You should not be concerned with how you look or whether you are doing it correctly. Let it become like an improvisational dance in which you express the content of your inner being. And, of course, don't forget to have lots of fun!

1. Stand on a stable surface with your feet shoulder-width apart. Bend your knees so that your hips lower slightly. Allow your arms to drop forward slightly, and relax your shoulders completely.

2. Close your eyes and begin to bounce your hips up and down, following a rhythm that feels natural for your body.

3. Focus on exhaling and releasing tension from your body. Continue bouncing gently for 5 or more minutes until your body feels fully relaxed.

4. When you are fully relaxed, begin to follow your own vibration. There is no right or wrong posture at this point—just follow what feels natural to you. The vibration may be intense or gentle, depending on your particular needs. You may feel compelled to make dance-like movements as well.

5. As you return to full consciousness, shake out your arms and legs. Breathe in deeply, exhale fully, and sweep down your arms and torso with your palms.

VARIATIONS OF BRAIN WAVE VIBRATION

These postures are specially designed to work with the flow of energy of the body for deep healing of problems that are common to most people in modern society. Many of them are especially well suited for centering your energy and for reversing the effects of stress in the body.

Most of us, because of stress, sedentary lifestyle, and busy minds, have something of an upside-down energy condition. Ideally, your energy should be centered in the lower abdomen, but if you are like most people, your energy is more concentrated in the head. This leads to various common conditions, like headaches, insomnia, high blood pressure, and digestive problems. Including these exercises as part of your daily routine will help you return your energy system to a more healthy state.

The first two can be used as a way to warm up before Full-Body Brain Wave Vibration. Eventually, as your ability to evaluate your own energy conditions improves, you can also create your own variations, but in the meantime, you can give these time-tested versions a try.

Chest Twist Vibration

This exercise helps release tension from the chest area, which is usually hard to stretch completely through ordinary stretching exercises. It is a good choice when you feel burdened by emotions because it works to open up the chest, which is where we tend to hold emotions like sadness and disappointment. Chest Twist Vibration is also effective for relieving lung problems, such as asthma or bronchitis. During this exercise, focus on moving the chest, not just the arms.

When you first begin this exercise you may feel some pain in the body, which indicates that you have some blockage. Discomfort of this sort is most prevalent in the sides beneath the rib cage and in the spine, but it could be anywhere in the body. If the pain is extremely severe, you should stop, but otherwise it is best to power through the pain to help open the blockage.

1. Stand with your feet parallel and shoulder-width apart. Relax your body completely, breathe comfortably, and close your eyes. Bend your knees slightly and release all tension.

2. Lift your elbows out to the side and place your hands in front of the middle of your chest. Face your palms toward the ground, but keep your hands, shoulders, and arms relaxed. Bend your knees slightly.

3. Twist your torso from side to side, as though you are spinning on an axis. Twist only your upper body, keeping your hips and thighs completely stationary. Breathe in deeply and exhale completely.

4. Continue the motion for several minutes. If you feel pain, breathe into the pain, focusing on directing fresh, healing energy into the area that feels painful. Continue until the motion feels comfortable. After a few minutes, let your arms drop, allowing them to swing side to side.

Abdominal Vibration

This form of Brain Wave Vibration, also known as Dahn-jon Clapping, will help facilitate incredible improvements to your health if you practice it regularly. Abdominal Vibration is among the most effective methods for improving the overall balance of energy in the body as it draws heat energy away from the head and into the abdomen.

This is a classic exercise to begin to stimulate the physical energy of the body. The physical energy is centered in the lower abdomen in what is called the *lower Dahn-jon*, but many of us, usually because of inactivity, do not have strong lower Dahn-jons. This is a way to reinvigorate the lower Dahn-jon, and thus the physical body as well.

If you suffer from any digestive problems, you should practice this consistently, working up to 1,000 repetitions per day. It is a good idea to do 100 to 200 repetitions at the beginning of any Brain Wave Vibration session in order to stabilize and center your energy. This exercise can also be completed in a variety of postures, including lying on your back or on your side. As you shift position, you will notice a difference in the sensation as it targets different parts of the body. If small black-and-blue marks appear on your abdomen, don't worry—it is normal and will disappear after a few days of practice.

1. Shake out your arms and legs to relax completely. Stand with your feet parallel and shoulder-width apart. Bend your knees slightly.

2. Curl your pelvis upward so that you feel a slight tension in the lower abdomen. Focus your mind on the area a couple of inches below your navel and two inches inside the body.

3. Cup your hands slightly and begin to rhythmically strike the lower abdomen area with both palms.

4. Begin with 100 strikes. You may increase the number and force of the strikes as you progress.

Toe-Tap Vibration

This is another form of Brain Wave Vibration that can help heal many physical problems, including headaches, insomnia, and circulation problems. Like Abdominal Vibration, Toe-Tap Vibration helps return the body's energy balance to a healthy state by bringing energy down to the lower body. It is also a very good mind-body coordination exercise.

Toe-Tap Vibration is also a great brain-body coordination exercise. Because the feet are so far away from the brain, you may find that at first they do not want to cooperate! But keep working at it and keep trying to increase your speed and the evenness of the rhythm.

The feet also contain a wide variety of acupressure points that are stimulated during this exercise. Because all the energy lines in the body end in the feet, you can energize your whole body when you stimulate your feet.

1. Lie down on the floor comfortably. Place your arms and legs on the floor and close your eyes. Breathe in and out several times to release excess tension.
2. As you are lying there, gently shake your head from side to side, allowing your shoulders, arms, legs, and your whole body to relax. Imagine that all your stress is melting into the ground.

3. Inhale through your nose and exhale through your mouth, making a whooshing sound.

4. Repeat this 3 times.

5. Touch your heels together, tap your toes together, then part the toes again, trying to touch the sides of the feet on the ground. Repeat several times in quick succession. Adjust speed on the motion depending on comfort level, but repeat at least 50 times without stopping.

6. When you begin to feel fatigued, slowly stop tapping and rest. Feel the subtle vibration going through the end of the toes to the knees, thighs, hips, and waist and to the top of the head. Challenge yourself to do a greater number of repetitions each time you practice.

Energy Meditation

This exercise will help you learn to sense the presence of energy. Its traditional name, Ji-gam, means "stop thinking," and this is essentially the goal—to stop thinking. It requires deep, relaxed concentration, the perfect remedy for stressed-out brains. You should be as relaxed as possible before attempting this exercise, so stretch your body or use other forms of Brain Wave Vibration before you begin. At first, the feeling might be subtle. Do your best to clear your mind and focus on that sensation. If you find it difficult to feel the sensation, try clapping your hands several times before increasing sensitivity. Keep practicing this, and soon you will find that the sensation grows stronger.

1. Sit comfortably on the floor or on a chair, and straighten your back.
2. Place your hands on your knees with your palms facing up and close your eyes. Relax your body, especially your neck and shoulders. Inhale deeply; let go of any remaining tension while exhaling. (Soft meditative music in the background may be helpful.)
3. Raise your hands slowly to chest level, with your palms facing each other but not touching. First concentrate on any sensation you may feel between your palms.

4. Now allow about 2–4 inches of space between your hands and concentrate fully on the space. Imagine that your shoulders, arms, wrists, and hands are floating in a vacuum, weightless.

5. Pull your hands apart and push them closer together again as you maintain your concentration. You may feel a tingling sensation or a magnetic attraction pulling your hands toward each other or pushing them apart.

6. When the sensation becomes more real, pull your hands farther apart or push them closer together. The sensation will expand and become stronger.

7. Breathe in and out, slowly and deeply, 3 times. Rub your hands together briskly until they are warm, then gently sweep your palms over your face, neck, and chest.

Energy Dance

This exercise, also known as Dahn-mu, will increase your energy awareness while also releasing your natural inner grace and expressiveness. It is also very healing, as your body will take postures that will help realign the body and improve circulation. You should develop some ability in the previous exercise, the Energy Meditation, before attempting this. In the third step of Brain Wave Vibration, you may find that your body naturally moves into this Energy Dance.

Begin by follow the directions for the Energy Meditation on page 194.

Focusing on the palms, allow your hands to follow the flow of energy freely. Allow your body to be enveloped by the energy and move accordingly, free from inhibition and restriction.

Jang-saeng Walking

Walking is a natural way to bring rhythmic vibrations to your body, which perhaps is why it is so healthful and refreshing. With every step, you send a wave of energy through your body. Jang-saeng Walking capitalizes on this by adjusting the posture of the body for ideal energy flow. The word *jang-saeng* means "longevity," and that is what this exercise is meant to produce.

1. Walk with feet parallel while putting strength on *Yong-chun*, an energy point located at the ball of the foot, and on the toes.
2. Tuck the tailbone upward and tighten your lower abdomen. As you walk, lean forward slightly, tilting forward about one degree.
3. Walk with an open chest. Breathe naturally into the abdomen, being sure to exhale completely.
4. Walk with a bright smile. Walk with a sense of purpose and forward momentum.
5. Swing both arms freely as you walk.
6. Feel subtle vibrations spreading throughout the soles, chest, and the entire body.

Surfing the Wave of Life

Now that you have learned to reconnect to the rhythm of your own body and mind through Brain Wave Vibration, you can view the universe as a vast ocean of endless possibility. Remember that your whole life is but a wave on that ocean. Your every thought and action adds momentum and direction to your wave. It is up to you to determine at which shore your life will arrive.

Approach your life the way a surfer faces the ocean. I have heard that a surfer must wipe out hundreds of times before ever having a really great ride. But all of those moments of failure teach the rider something about balance—not really something you could write in a book but a feeling, a way of harmonizing with the wave. If you seek this sort of harmony with everything life brings, there can be no failure.

At times, when you are out in the middle of the sea of life, you may feel lonely and afraid. You have no reason to fear, however, if you simply keep connected to the vibrations of the universe and the source of life. Brain Wave Vibration exists to help you keep connected to the cosmos simply and without much effort. Through it, you can discover your purest mind and your highest ideals so that you can live for the betterment of all humanity. In other words, it can help you be true to who you really are inside.

Please listen carefully to the song that is coming from within your soul; it is a song of peace and a song of hope. It is telling you that everything you really want will come to you. It is telling you that your potential is greater than even the widest of seas. Your brain is waiting, like the North Star, to guide you to your destination.

I hope also that you will have the courage to face greater and greater waves during your life. There is no joy in riding safely in the protected waters of a bay. You must be willing to challenge yourself in order to achieve the life you want.

As you ride the wave of your life, look ahead to the waves that are coming, but keep yourself in harmony with the moment. The wave will go up, and the wave will go down. Either way, realize the natural beauty of this and learn to always be grateful. This is the source of lasting joy.

Appendixes

Stories of Healing and Hope

Ilchi Lee says that the work that he does is meant to provide people with three essential elements: health, happiness, and peace.
Brain Wave Vibration is especially notable among the hundreds
of techniques that he has developed because of its profound simplicity and surprising level of effectiveness. For that reason, he
has traveled widely, teaching the technique to people in Korea,
Japan, and the United States. Thousands of people worldwide
have benefited from Brain Wave Vibration, and many inspiring stories have emerged—enough to fill a book of their own.
People have found relief for everything from chronic diseases to
personal relationship problems. In the next few pages, you will
meet some of the people making physical, mental, and spiritual
changes in their lives with the help of Brain Wave Vibration.

For Your Health

The first changes often occur on the physical level. Even if you
don't have any specific health issues, you are likely to be amazed

at the relaxation and the increased energy that you feel. We have heard about recovery from an incredible array of ailments: high blood pressure, headache, chronic fatigue, multiple sclerosis, reproductive problems, obesity, and skin conditions, just to name a few. Of course, Brain Wave Vibration is not meant to replace medical care, but it is clear that it can greatly assist the body in the process of recovery.

Stress

There is no question that stress is an underlying cause of so many health problems in today's world. Release from the vicious cycle of stress and tension is at the root of all healing experienced through Brain Wave Vibration. Even if stress-related health problems have not yet appeared, many people report feeling more relaxed and less stressed.

> When I started doing Brain Wave Vibration, I wondered if it was just a gimmick. How could something so easy create long-term benefits? After experiencing it just a few times, I changed my opinion. It has helped me manage my chronic pain, increase my energy level, and improve my attitude about life in general. In just a short time, my quality of life has improved, and I know it will continue to improve as I progress in my training.
>
> —Leslie A. Mamalis, Lakewood, CO

Starting the day this way is a special gift to my body, mind, and soul. Through Brain Wave Vibration—moving my body, following my rhythm, and stopping my busy mind—I am able to connect and heal my body and mind. It is absolutely one of the most effective techniques I've experienced for purifying my whole body, clearing my mind, and nurturing the spirit. It's simple to do and allows me to deeply connect within, listen to my body choose, create, and achieve what I want. Amazing!

—*Helen Nelson, Kipling, CO*

I think Brain Wave Vibration is helping me a lot—I feel energized, I feel lighter, and my brain wakes up a lot, which is helpful because I do research and writing a lot. After yoga practice my body and brain are stress free and very light. My neck pain is relieved.

—*Ayesha Yasmin, Franklin Square, NY*

Pain

Chronic pain is often described as an "epidemic" by health care professionals because so many people are suffering with it daily. Brain Wave Vibration is founded on the principle that pain or illness of any kind is a sign of imbalance in the body. People find relief from pain as they begin to reestablish the natural equilibrium of their bodies, even in cases where pharmaceuticals and other treatments have failed to provide relief.

I suffered from pains in the neck and shoulders as I sat at the computer all day. After I started Brain Wave Vibration, the shoulders and the neck became soft and relaxed. After only ten minutes of exercise, I can really feel the difference.

—*Cecile Kohoei, Mesa, AZ*

Five years ago when I first experienced Brain Wave Vibration I was in constant pain. My lower back was sore all the time, and my knees hurt so that I was forced to limp and to hold on to furniture just to get around. When I saw the instructor and the participants start vibration exercise, I thought, "That looks easy," and I decided to give it a try. At first, there was some pain, but it soon diminished. Now I just have fun! I feel so much better! Because of this vibration class I do things I never thought I could do!

—*Carol Scholl, Kirkland, WA*

As I was shaking my head, I felt a painful popping and crackling on the side of my head. After just a few minutes the pain and crackling disappeared. My neck feels warm and flexible—which is unusual, since it is normally rather stiff and painful—especially on the right side.

—*Nancy Davis, Springfield, VA*

Even after years of training to be a yoga instructor, I had a lot of trouble sitting cross-legged. I had injured my hip joint a long time ago, and it was usually stiff and tense. Often, when

I would sit cross-legged in front of the class, my students appeared more flexible than I was. After doing Brain Wave Vibration in a seated position, my hip joints have opened significantly. Sitting posture is now much more comfortable, and I can meditate much more deeply than before.

—David Driscoll, Orland Park, IL

Fatigue

"I feel more energized" is one of the most common comments reported by practitioners. The reason for this is simple. Once stress and tension has been released from the body, the ki energy is finally able to flow freely around the body.

I have been doing Brain Wave Vibration diligently during the past three months. First of all, I feel more energized. Even with less sleep, I spring from bed in the morning.

—Kyung Yon Lee, Korea

Since I began traveling more intensely for business, I have made Brain Wave Vibration part of my travel routine. The act of moving my body, beginning with the simple nodding of my head, is then followed by vibrations down my spine, which allows me to relieve the tension that gathers in my neck, shoulders , and upper back after a day of meetings and working at my computer.

—Brenna McCormick, Arlington, MA

Blood Pressure

Asian medical models state that, to remain healthy, a person's warm (fire) energy should pool in the abdomen and cool (water) energy should circulate to the head. High blood pressure is a sure sign that the opposite is true, that hot energy is collecting in the head. By quieting the mind and releasing stress from the body, Brain Wave Vibration helps return the body to a healthier energetic state, thereby normalizing blood pressure.

I was rushed to the emergency room in the middle of the night because my blood pressure shot up so high. After I started Brain Wave Vibration, however, not only did my blood pressure improve, my vision has improved and my headaches are gone. My head also feels clear and light. Two minutes of simple head shaking helps my vision become clearer. Unlike other exercises, Brain Wave Vibration is easy to do even while watching TV.

—Young Sook Park, Korea

I have had high blood pressure for over forty years. Before Brain Wave Vibration my blood pressure was about 150 over 89. This was while being on three different medications for blood pressure. My new blood pressure readings have been as low as 106 over 76. This is nothing short of a miracle!

—Ron Cohen, Utica, MI

Headaches

Headaches, like high blood pressure, are a sign that too much heat energy is gathering in the head. Our culture is the perfect breeding ground for headaches because we are constantly inundated with information, and our minds become full of all sorts of random thoughts and images. Brain Wave Vibration helps quiet the mind so that the energy can stay lower in the body and headaches can be relieved.

> Since beginning Brain Wave Vibration, my head feels lighter and I am able to think more clearly. Now I do not get migraines, and I am less stressed in general.
>
> *—Annette M. Ahlers, Washington, DC*

> I have been doing Brain Wave Vibration over a month now and have experienced unexpected changes in my body. Now the horrible headaches that would visit me from time to time and knock me down are under control. The headache always hit me at any time that I was lacking sleep or or was under stress. Once the headache was ignited and was running its course, the pain escalated to full burning flames and then died down. So whenever I experienced the early sign of a headache, I would attempt stretching, walking, sleeping, and painkillers to deaden the pain—but it was to no avail.
>
> Not too long ago, I started doing Brain Wave Vibration at the first sign of a headache. To my surprise, the pain did

not escalate beyond a certain point. So I repeated Brain Wave Vibration every two hours. As a result, I finally became free from the headache by the end of the day. I got rid of even the remaining smolder of pain with Brain Wave Vibration exercise.

—In Young Oh, Korea

There were two times in the last week that I felt the oncoming headache symptoms in the right side of my head. The Brain Wave Vibration method enabled me to release the feeling and prevent the migraine from occurring.

—Stephanie Saxon, Honolulu, HI

Sensory Problems

The five senses are like information portals to the brain. Through them, our brain interacts with the world around us. When something goes wrong with sight, smell, hearing, touch, or taste, it is like we have been cut off from our world. And unfortunately, once lost, senses can be very difficult to regain. Nevertherless, several people have reported improvements in this area.

I was born with a condition called "amblyopia," or "lazy eye." My left eye is much weaker than my right eye, which causes misalignment of the eyes. I have had to wear corrective lenses for this condition for my whole life. Recently, after having practiced Brain Wave Vibration for a while, I broke my glasses. It was only then that I realized how much my eyes had improved.

—*Nathan Guadagni, West Linn, OR*

Due to a brain injury, I had not had a sense of smell since 1981. After twenty months of Brain Wave Vibration, I walked outside one day to find that it had just started to rain. To my amazement, I could smell that subtle smell that is present when it starts to rain. Not only that, I could smell the corn roasting at the Cowboy festival that was happening down the street. It was just wonderful.

—*Maxie Bilikie, Sedona. AZ*

After our first class, the numbness in my thumb, index, and middle fingers was almost totally gone. Moreover, my eyesight has improved to the point where, when I drive home, I no longer need to wear my glasses. I even forget to put them on!

—*Noel Johnson, Cambridge, MA*

I noticed in September that I had about five floaters in my right eye. I put in the audio training CD and did Brain Wave Vibration for about ten minutes. I have done that every day and my floaters have almost totally disappeared.

—*Martha E. McKinley, Kekaha, HI*

Chronic Disease

Some of the most amazing stories come from people suffering from progressively debilitating diseases. When conventional medicine cannot offer much relief, it is easy for these sufferers to give up the hope of ever returning to a state of real health. But Brain Wave Vibration offers them a new chance to search deeply into their body's natural healing ability, and often the results are quite amazing.

> I suffer from multiple sclerosis. I had to wear feet support in the socks and use a cane simply to walk. I could not move my feet for three years. Now I can lift my feet. I can even move furniture without help. Before, I fell out of balance when I pulled my head backward. Not anymore! Even my doctor is very surprised.
>
> —*Sharon M. Everett, Mesa, AZ*

> My health was significantly compromised. I was severely anemic, my kidneys weren't functioning properly, and the medical professionals wanted me to be on chemotherapy, but my liver was creating complications. I was experiencing a lot of pain in my musculoskeletal system, and I wasn't sleeping much more than two hours a night. I was kind of a mess. I am now doing great, and all these physical ailments are completely gone! The Brain Wave Vibration technique specifically helped me sleep more effectively and keep my emotions balanced and positive so that I could truly heal

my physical body. This technique, combined with others from Dahn Yoga, has probably been the primary contributor to my healing, and I am so grateful.

—*Laura Anderson, Scottsdale, AZ*

When I started Brain Wave Vibration five months ago, I had intense fibromyalgia pain throughout my body. Today I can honestly say that I have no pain whatsoever. It has helped me become more balanced, focused, and strong as well. It is the best thing that could ever be. I feel that it keeps my brain happy, centered, and alive.

—*Yolanda Jaramillo, Mesa, AZ*

A year and a half ago, I was diagnosed with multiple sclerosis. After 8-9 months of practice, I went in for a medical exam. To my doctor's surprise, brain lesions disappeared from my MRI scan. He said this could not have been the medication I was taking. Also, I got half an inch taller!

—*Debbie Nelson, Mesa, AZ*

I have been suffering with fibromyalgia for twelve years. The fatigue was debilitating; I was not functioning, and it was beginning to wear me down. The benefits of Brain Wave Vibration were immediate for me. My fatigue disappeared and my pain decreased. Now, I am off medication, and my whole outlook on life has changed for the better.

—*Dianne Yates, West Linn, OR*

I had been struggling with fibromyaglia and arthritis in my joints. I was taking medications as well as getting cortisone shots in my neck and shoulder, but nothing seemed to help. I felt worse after every treatment! My daughter could see that I was suffering and she wanted me to feel better but without taking so many pills. After all this, I was also beginning to loose my balance. I had trouble staying steady on my feet, and I couldn't walk up stairs without support. The pain and frustration was really getting to me. I decided I would try this one last thing. Then I took several classes called Brain Wave Vibration. Almost immediately I felt my body change. I could feel energy moving in a way I had never felt before. The next day, I didn't feel as much pain in my body, and it was amazing!

The Brain Wave Vibration class helped me change the way I felt in my body and also change the way I felt about my body. With the help of Brain Wave Vibration, I have stopped taking pain medication. I'm not tired or depressed now, I don't need pain medication to get me through the day. My family is thrilled with the new me.

—Angela Pisa, Andover, MA

Other Ailments

Brain Wave Vibration practitioners have found relief from a wide variety of physical problems. As your body returns to a state of balance, you too will uncover your natural healing ability.

After starting Brain Wave Vibration, my sinuses cleared and my headaches ceased. Also, when I was young I went to rock concerts, which resulted in a loud ringing in the ears. Since I started, it has subsided considerably. Now it is just a faint whisper, and I suspect one day it will be gone completely.

—Toni Graves, West Linn, OR

When the weather was hot, I suffered from skin rashes on the arms, legs, neck—wherever the skin folds. This summer, however, I did not experience any skin problem. Just think about that—I had suffered skin problems for thirty-six long years. On top of that, I had to apply oil to the hands and feet in winter because of bleeding from chapped skin. Now my hands and feet are moist and soft, thanks to Brain Wave Vibration.

—Hwa Kil Park, Korea

The doctor wanted me to go on medication for bone loss, but I refused. After ten months of Brain Wave Vibration, I went back to the doctor for more tests, and much to my doctor's surprise, my bone density increased 3.8 percent. The doctor told me that studies have shown that vibration is good for the bones.

—Sharon Gardner, Westminster, CO

When I started this practice, I certainly didn't expect much relief from my diverticulitis, since I thought there was nothing that could be done for it. In fact, my doctor told me it was time to consider having a foot of my colon removed. However, through Brain Wave Vibration, I have learned to strengthen my abdomen and to bring heat to the area. My abdomen is now much stronger, and the diverticulitis has completely disappeared.

—Kathy Hallock, Honolulu, HI

I am 90 years old. Today is my fourth Brain Wave Vibration session and already I've changed my flexibility a lot and have more stamina and better balance. Now I can do one-finger push-ups against the wall. I think everyone needs to experience this training.

—David Hill, Moraga center, CA

Several years ago, I was diagnosed with chronic bronchitis and emphysema. I have had to sleep using an oxygen tank, and whenever I exerted myself I had to rely on a portable oxygen tank. After two months of Brain Wave Vibration, I no longer use my portable unit when I exert myself, and I now enjoy the freedom of exercise without the use of the oxygen tank.

—Suzanne Einhorn, Houston, TX

Case Studies

Through the following stories, you will see in detail how physical ailments can disrupt a person's life. You will also see that no matter how desperate the situation, things can turn around quickly if you give the body a chance. In the first story, you will meet a woman, now on the road to recovery, whose life was completely derailed after sustaining a painful injury.

Ten years ago, I was injured while helping my coworkers lift a woman who had a seizure. I ended up having neck disk surgery, and a disk pin was placed in my neck. This was never comfortable, but then last year things really got bad. I suddenly started having pain all over my body, as though my entire nervous system was affected.

Eventually it got so bad that I could not function at work, and I was hospitalized for a while. I tried many drugs, including cortisone, but nothing helped much. Fortunately, the first day away from work, I happened to pass a Dahn Yoga Center. I had taken tai chi before and loved it, so I was interested in giving it a try. Because I was in such bad shape, I decided to take private healing sessions, which focused on Brain Wave Vibration as a healing method.

I experienced the benefits of Brain Wave Vibration right away. In the early stages, I felt like something was shifting in my body. My body really wanted to get better, and somehow the vibrations were helping unleash something from deep inside. With each session, I became stronger and stronger.

Now I am virtually pain free for the first time in a long time, and I am able to walk and enjoy my life as normal. Whenever I feel pain, all I have to do is take ten minutes to feel the rhythm of my own body. It has shifted my whole outlook on the experience of stress and pain in my body and has given me a real sense of control over these things. I think of Brain Wave Vibration as my "balancer." Even other people have noticed how much calmer and centered I am. All in all, Brain Wave Vibration has been an awesome experience for me.

—Linda Mazur, West Linn, OR

Buddhist monastic life is devoted to the contemplation of spiritual ideals. But as this nun's story shows, you must first have a healthy body to have a healthy spirit.

I have devoted myself to Koan meditation training at a small temple that was left to me by my grandfather. Koan is a Buddhist training method intended to help one gain realization, a method I practiced for a long time.

About six years ago, I got night polyuria, a condition that causes one to urinate frequently during the night. It is caused by kidney failure. I would have to go to the bathroom at least four, and as many as seven, times per night.

Because I could not sleep well at night, I was always tired during the day. I had all sorts of medications. I also suffered from severe back pain caused by the renal failure, and it was difficult for me to go on with my training. I felt like my body was falling asleep and felt coldness throughout my body. When I went to a hospital to get a checkup, they told me that I had six benign tumors. The doctor told me that I had to have the largest ones surgically removed.

After the surgery, someone recommended Brain Wave Vibration to me, so I started the training as a member at a Dahn Yoga Center. The first day, I learned Dahn-jon Clapping (Abdominal Vibration, page 190) and practiced Brain Wave Vibration for about twenty minutes. I was skeptical at first, but I put my mind on the vibration and practiced hard.

I was very tired on the way back to the temple on the first day. But that night, I didn't wake up even once all night. Amazingly, I had solved my six years of night polyuria in only one night. I felt completely refreshed and full of energy. I couldn't believe it.

It is not only my body that has improved through Brain Wave Vibration. I finally gained an answer for the koan that I was trying to understand for so long. I felt like some part of my brain was opening up and connecting with something. I started feeling true joy. My mind became happy, just like that of a child. I am now thinking about how I am going to share this realization and happiness with others.

I practiced Dahn-jon Clapping and Brain Wave Vibration whenever I had time. About a month after I started practicing at the Dahn Yoga Center, I went back to the doctor to have a checkup, and he was truly amazed. He said that all the tumors were gone except for a very small one. As I heard him say this, I thought, "Now I can live."

Brain Wave Vibration gave me health and a new lease on life. I finally gained an answer for the philosophical puzzle I had been trying to solve for a long time. I finally understand what Buddha meant when he said: "Find truth in your body; outside you will not find it in a thousand years."

—*Seong Deok, Korea*

For Your Happiness

One might say that without happiness there can be no health. Our emotions and attitudes, in fact, may be the foundation of our well-being. Here you can read about practitioners of Brain Wave Vibration who have improved their mental health along with their physical health. Many have found centeredness within themselves and have gained control over the emotions that have negative effects on their lives. People improve their personal relationships, they overcome depression, and they are able to break debilitating, negative habits. And, after only a few weeks of training, most people report improved focus and cognitive skill. All of this adds up to a happier, more fulfilling life.

Focus

Lack of ability to concentrate is probably one of the most common mental problems of modern society. With so many distractions, it is a wonder that anyone can concentrate on anything. Brain Wave Vibration can help you build your ability to focus by clearing out the static in your brain caused by the constant bombardment of information.

> For me, it is a quiet time, even with the sound of vibrating drums, a time to quiet my mind without interruption from my thoughts. The healing vibration stays with me throughout the day. Taking three minutes at home to practice Brain Wave Vibration brings me back into balance again.
>
> —Dawn Skong, Springfield, VA

> Brain Wave Vibration helps me clear my mind and focus on what I want to do. I'm able to put all the extraneous things out of my head for a little while.
>
> —Lauren Minto, Washington, DC

> No more lying awake for hours with all sorts of thoughts going through my head. I have been able to calm down my brain waves so that I don't have thoughts running through my brain every night, and I am able to keep positive thoughts.
>
> —Betsy Butler, Lakewood, CO

Memory

Good memory skill is the offspring of good focus. If you find yourself becoming a little forgetful, it is probably not because there is something wrong with your brain. Rather, it is simply because your mind is too cluttered to allow things to stick. Here are a couple of people who improved their memory through Brain Wave Vibration.

> I was preparing for my graduate school entrance exam. It required memorizing a few pages of conversation written in Chinese. I was nervous, but, making my brain lighter with Brain Wave Vibration, I managed to stay calm and clear. Needless to say, I passed the exam.
>
> *—Jee-ae Ahn, Korea*

> With Brain Wave Vibration, I'm just clearer. During the day, I remember what I need to remember. I find that I don't need to write as many notes to myself.
>
> *—Barbara Brooks, Mesa, AZ*

Emotional Control

Brain Wave Vibration helps you gain control of your emotions by first allowing you to let go of negative emotional patterns.

> When first beginning Brain Wave Vibration, I realized that there was this natural movement in my body. Now that I

fully understand the brain wave training, my body responds in different ways. I will say that I continually smile; I feel lighter overall; I feel just amazing. It's been at least ten years since I have felt this good, and at twenty-three, I never thought I would have this feeling.

—*Amanda Leddy, West Bloomfield, MI*

I used to try to suppress anger until it exploded, which made me difficult to get along with. With Brain Wave Vibration, I was able to feel and watch oppressed emotions building up. I completely cleansed ill feelings from my system with profuse tears. Now my understanding of myself has deepened, and I have gained an ability to look at myself objectively.

—*Sung Ah Hong, Korea*

I believe Brain Wave Vibration saved my life. I felt very depressed and unhappy. I started classes three months ago, and my life has changed. Brain Wave Vibration made me happy, improved my attitude, and gave me more energy.

—*Candy Dockstader, Lakewood, CO*

Most of the time, I'm happier and calmer since starting Brain Wave Vibration. If I let a little of that old habit of worry sneak in, I just do a little brain vibration. Then my brain kicks in and reminds me that everything will work out, even if I don't know how.

—*Nadea Collins, Mesa, AZ*

I had been taking anti-depression pills for six years when I first came to the Dahn Yoga Center. My purpose wasn't to cure my depression, but only to find a healthier way of life. However, after a few weeks of practice, I felt so much happier and stronger that I decided to cut my daily pill in half, to see if I could reduce the quantity of medicine I was absorbing.

After only three months of regular practice I had completely quit taking my pills! I call it a miracle, but the Dahn Yoga Instructors prefer to say that through Brain Wave Vibration, I found the key to unlocking the self-healing power that was already inside me.

—Céline Auffret, Hoboken, NJ

My grandmother had recently passed away, and I was having a hard time letting go of her. I also had a lifetime of anger towards my mother. During Brain Wave Vibration I could see a very clear image of my grandmother slowly floating away. At first, I tried to hang on to her, but then I let go. The next thing I know, my mother is standing right next to me. I automatically opened my arms to her, forgiving her for all the things I held for all those years. It is probably just the beginning of my healing, but I'll take that and continue practicing Brain Wave Vibration.

—Wendy Ormsby, Beltsville, MD

Habits

Brain Wave Vibration can also help you break debilitating be-havior patterns. While you are practicing, you will also be more open to your own positive suggestions, as these people were.

I could never wake up with my alarm. While doing Brain Wave Vibration, just moving my head back and forth, I said to myself, "I will get up when the alarm goes off." And the next morning, I did! Every time I have tried this before going to bed, it has worked.

—Leanne Garn, Kirkland, WA

I was overweight. Wrong eating habits were the main reasons. Meals were irregular, and I often overate, which eventually weakened my digestive system. My body and mind were not in good shape. Once I continued to do Brain Wave Vibration ten minutes every day, I began to lose weight, and my appetite was subdued. I finally managed to eat regularly only as much as I needed.

—Jae Yol Yoon, Korea

Twenty-one days after starting Brain Wave Vibration, I quit a forty-year smoking habit. I feel good about myself more than anything else because I delivered on the promise I made to myself.

—Hong Kwan Ryu, Korea

Case Studies

To see how deeply transformational Brain Wave Vibration can be, it is helpful to see a person's change in the context of his or her complete life situation. Let's start with the story of a woman whose life was put on hold by postpartum depression and degenerative disk disease.

> Three years ago, after the birth of my son, I went into severe postpartum depression, which was accompanied by paralyzing bouts of anxiety. On top of that, I had degenerative disk disease in my spine. My neck was so stiff that I couldn't even look down and touch my chin on my chest. I had headaches all the time, and I heard crunching and creaking sounds whenever I moved my head. I could barely take proper care of my three-year-old son. I was a real mess, basically nonfunctional. The doctor gave me medication, but it caused terrible side effects, and it didn't help anyway.
>
> When I came to the Dahn Yoga Center, I was really at the end of my rope. I began doing Brain Wave Vibration sessions three times a week. I was amazed how quickly I progressed. After only one month, my spine gained so much flexibility I was able to bend over and touch my toes. And, for the first time in my life, I can touch my chin to my chest! This is something most people may take for granted, but for me it is like a gift.
>
> *–Julie Eggen, West Linn, OR*

Being a police officer is perhaps one of the most stressful jobs around. This is the story of one who was able to find emotional stability despite his difficult and psychologically exhausting job.

I am a cop. My workplace is the police station, where all sorts of conflicts between people happen. The environment is always discordant. When I get tired, my facial expression becomes just like my workplace. And then I feel even worse when I spit out words of frustration with a stern face.

The most stressful moments at my work are when I am misunderstood by people while I am trying to calm them down and make peace. Sometimes they insult me without any reason, which I take personally. Most of the time, I just let it go. But there are moments when I cannot take it anymore. On days like that, I cannot rest well, even after I get off work. All the negativity and the hostile words linger in my head. I guess it is an occupational hazard. I thought I would become seriously ill if I kept going on like that.

Even before I learned Brain Wave Vibration, I started shaking my head left and right after I interrogated people. I think my neck and shoulders were trying to revive themselves of all that stress and stiffness. One day, a friend of mine introduced me to Brain Wave Vibration at a Dahn Yoga Center, and I could easily follow all the motions, as they were similar to the ones I used to do. I didn't notice a big difference at the beginning of the exercise, but I started feeling my head becoming clearer after about twenty minutes.

As I rode on the rhythm of my body, all those negative feelings that were giving me a hard time disappeared.

After I experienced this, whenever I felt unpleasant I started shaking the negativity off immediately by doing Brain Wave Vibration. I decided to delete my negative feelings right away. In the beginning, it was not easy to do. But after I practiced several times, I could easily control my feelings by shaking my neck and body, even if just a little bit.

Recently, I began to actively imagine what I wanted myself to be during Brain Wave Vibration. I visualize all the negativity and hostility being eliminated, which helps my body become even more refreshed and energized. I still may feel upset at an accident scene, but I immediately practice Brain Wave Vibration on the way back in the patrol car. My method is to rub my hands together and stroke my head with my hands, and then delete those unpleasant feelings by shaking my head. When my fellow cops have a hard time with difficult emotional memories, I shout at them and laugh, "Delete it!"

—Jin-hwan Kim, Korea

For Your Peacefulness

If you are willing to go deeply enough into your practice, you may come to some epiphanies about the world and your place in it, as this group of stories demonstrates. Connecting to energy greater than your own personal energy, you too will be able to see the big picture of your life and gain a better sense of meaning and purpose. Take your practice time as a precious moment with yourself. Get to know who you are and where you fit in the grand scheme of the universe.

Healthy Information

Brain Wave Vibration seems to allow people to take a deeper look at themselves and the things holding them back. These people were all able to transcend information about themselves, gaining the ability to step forward in life.

> The biggest change that happened to me is I ran completely out of the limiting information that used to confine me. When I ran out of negative information, I sensed that something had changed in my brain. Since then, whenever I encounter a knotty problem, I try to get an answer through Brain Wave Vibration.
>
> —*Kyung-hee Im, Korea*

> I came to realize that I had been too conscious of other people's views of me. I put myself in a frame, telling myself, "You must always look cheerful," "You must be polite," "You must be nice." In a word, I lived in a tight frame

of "dos and don'ts." If I didn't live up to those standards, I habitually punished myself. Now, I no longer disparage myself by comparing myself to others. I love myself the way I am. It is a wonderful feeling.

—Jee Young Nam, Korea

One day while doing the Brain Wave Vibration exercise, I began to feel "another me" who was watching "me" who I always had been. The "old me" I was watching looked pathetic with lots of wounds from being kicked around in the course of life. I felt so sorry for myself that I cried out loud out of sympathy. And then I discovered there was something inside of me that made me distrust myself. That thing tried to make me believe that I lacked willpower and patience. The moment I realized the existence of such a negative element, it disappeared.

—Dae Suk Woo, Korea

I could not make the right notes of music with my voice. For example, "re" came out of my mouth when I attempted to make "do." I was reaching a point where I simply could not continue to sing. About one year after starting Brain Wave Vibration, I was finally able to hit the right notes and sing like I had when I was younger. It was like I turned around at the end of my career as a singer. I am so happy that I can sing again.

—Bum Yong Kim, Korea

Serenity

True peace is something that can come only from within. Many people have used Brain Wave Vibration to gain a genuine sense of calm centeredness. In the midst of the vibrations, you can find the calm center, like the eye in the center of the storm.

> When I practice, I feel closer and closer to my real self. It gives me freedom that connects my body and soul. My right brain becomes harmonized with my left brain in a state of complete calm, peace, and emptiness. Even in this day and age with all the turmoils and vicissitudes, it all becomes so clear to me.
>
> *—Peter Haddad, Epsom, England*

> I am in my seventies but very healthy. As soon as I wake up in the morning, I start the day with Brain Wave Vibration exercise with my husband. I can experience freedom of my soul after dancing Dahn-mu. I will enjoy the blessing of life until the moment I die. I am so thankful I live as a human.
>
> *—Yokoda, Japan*

> Doing Brain Wave Vibration has had a very noticeable positive change on my mood outside class. I feel more grounded and balanced. The world would be a better place if we all did this every day.
>
> *—Alex Swick, Kipling, CO*

Having been a victim of childhood abuse, I could not calm myself down, not even for a minute. I would move restlessly all day long, and I couldn't sit still. When I started Brain Wave Vibration, my body just kept going with no thought of time or anything else. My mind started to calm and to become empty. My body felt so light, like I was floating on air. When we stopped, my mind and body felt so different.

—Maggie Martin, Aurora, CO

Rediscovering Your True Self

During life, we place a lot of layers of identity over who we really are inside. You can use Brain Wave Vibration to shake off these false layers and get back to who you really are inside.

Brain Wave Vibration is a direct link to my inner being—my True Self. It is a form of cleansing and healing—physically, emotionally, and spiritually. Brain Wave Vibration connects me to my Divinity.

By utilizing my brain stem, I can access and project my deepest desires. I can see them with the purest of clarity. I can see my soul and love her profoundly. I can find my vision and direction. Brain Wave Vibration is a practice of no thought. I have experienced letting go and allowing the power of the cosmos to vibrate me. As an earth human, I am the link between my earth home and Cosmic Energy.

This experience assures me that my mind is Cosmic Mind. My energy is Cosmic Energy. My experience is a gift and a practice of sincerity and gratitude. My life is divine.

—*Memory Lamfers, Westminster, CO*

I have been attending Brain Wave Vibration training for more than two months on Saturdays and Sundays. At the beginning it took me a lot of effort to follow the rhythm of the music and to keep a balance; gradually my movements became spontaneous shortly after we started vibration.

When I do not control my body anymore, I feel that I enter the stream of energy, and the conventional sense of "me" disappears. There is just pure energy, and I am that energy. But it is not just a spiritual experience. In everyday life I feel that old pattern of thought, of responding to different situations, is gradually changing, and I have more compassion and more courage to meet life's challenges.

—*Zoga Royt, Flushing, NY*

Through Brain Wave Vibration, I am able to connect deep inside to my true nature. The first time I did it, I could truly see myself. I was able to step back and see both fear and power deep inside me. I could see the infinite power and potential I held. As a result, I became happier and developed a happier outlook on life.

—*Sara Chears, Naperville, IL*

Case Study

Even if you have great expectations for your future, life can be difficult and can shake your confidence. Here is the story of a young teacher who used Brain Wave Vibration to go deeply inside to gain unshakable belief in herself.

Throughout my college years, I never doubted that being a teacher was the perfect job for me. I was confident that I would be a great teacher when I went to work as a student teacher. When I finally graduated and went to the first school to work, I was full of pride, believing I was the perfect teacher. I thought that I had studied hard, and I had all the necessary elements to be a good teacher.

But I was soon driven to despair when I met students in real life. I had so much to teach them, but the students were not paying attention to me. I was having a hard time getting up in the morning because of fatigue accumulated during the previous day. "I am having such a hard time. Why is this happening?" I asked myself. This thought later changed to, "I don't think I am qualified to be a teacher. I should consider getting a different kind of job."

During that time, one of the more experienced teachers recommended that I get training to teach Brain Education to children. When I was first introduced to Brain Wave Vibration, I thought, "What's the point of just shaking the head?" In the beginning, I focused only on the head and neck during Brain Wave Vibration, but eventually the motion spread through my entire body. Then the next day, I was able to wake up in the morning by myself without the aid of an alarm.

Now I manage my mind and body through Brain Wave Vibration. What I realized after the sixty hours of Brain Education training is that there was nothing at all wrong with the students. I was the problem. I was not a happy person, and I was looking around at the students and the world with that unhappy attitude.

I became much happier after the training, and I wanted to share that happiness with others. My students looked so loving when I met them again, and I could communicate well with my students for the rest of the semester. Then I finally started to have hope that I might one day be able to become a truly good teacher to my students.

One day, a student came to me and said, "I used to think that I couldn't do anything before I met you. But now, I think I can do anything. Thank you so much, teacher!" As I heard this, I cried out loud. I was so happy and so grateful.

—*Ji-hyeon Shim, Korea*

For Your Loved Ones

Perhaps the greatest form of healing comes through healing others. So once you have gained physical, mental, and spiritual benefits for yourself, you can share your success with others to assist them in their healing process. In fact, you will find that this happens automatically. As your brain waves become healthier, you will naturally have a positive effect on others.

Relationships

As you become more aware of your own brain waves, you will also become more aware of others' brain waves. You will realize in a profoundly real way that we are all connected, especially through the energies that we transmit into the world. In becoming aware of these energy connections, you will break free of destructive patterns that undermine the relationships in our lives.

> I've noticed that as I become more calm, my teenage kids' behaviors and attitudes also improve. Even if I feel frustrated by their choices, I can use Brain Wave Vibration to come back to a place of serenity inside, which gives them more parental stability. Best of all, I am teaching them, by example, a better way of managing emotions.
>
> —Laurel Rudzik, Fullerton, CA

I'm enjoying the benefits of being calm and relaxed all of the time. My teenagers can't push me over the edge anymore, which is puzzling for them. They are also learning to relax and go with the flow.

—Jean Herman, Utica, MI

My coworkers were often blatantly cruel to me. Now, thanks to my practice, I am able to truly love my coworkers from deep inside me. It has helped me handle the emotions and positively transform the situation.

—Yasmin Asgarali, Ottawa, Canada

I had been overwhelmed with self-pity, sadness, and anger because my mother abandoned me when I was only one. I lived as an alcoholic for a long time until I took up Brain Wave Vibration exercise. After a few months, my oppressed heart was finally relieved with uncontrollable tears. At that point, I could not help but cry out, "Mom, I will forgive you." Now I am extremely happy because I am free from alcohol.

—Hamakada Emiko, Japan

Brain Wave Vibration has helped me get rid of a lot of old baggage that was affecting my current relationships. This practice helps keep me in the moment so that the old hurts of the past don't cast a shadow in the present.

—Lisa Peraza, Garden Grove, CA

I taught it to my children so they can focus on their home-work and handle the stresses of their day. I showed it to my husband so that he can shake off the pressures of the day and sleep better at night. Brain Wave Vibration is such a sim-ple, yet effective method that I recommend it to everyone.

—*Tracie Warren, Las Vegas, NV*

Case Studies

There is no greater gift than that of hope. Here is the amazing story of a woman who helped her handicapped daughter make incredible progress through Brain Wave Vibration.

After having practiced Brain Wave Vibration for a few weeks, I knew it was very helpful. In just those few weeks, I have found that my eyesight improved, I felt less stressed, and I have fewer headaches. These were all great results for me, but as I read the book and learned more, I began to wonder, "Could Brain Wave Vibration help my daughter?"

My daughter is nineteen years old and suffers from Rett syndrome, a genetic disorder that prevents children from developing normally. Although she is technically an adult, she is physically, emotionally, and mentally less developed than a three-year-old child. She cannot walk, talk in full sen-tences, or feed or dress herself. She has been in a wheel-chair for seven years and must wear diapers. Her behavior, like all Rett kids, is severely autistic; she rarely interacts with or responds to others.

Because she is completely physically disabled, I decided to take matters into my own hands. She cannot shake her own body, so I decided to shake it for her. I just place my hands on her body and shake, shake, shake! Also, I pat her body all over with my palms. She absolutely loves it!

After only one month of Brain Wave Vibration, I have seen incredible changes in my daughter. She has begun talking more and responds to me when I speak to her. She still wears her diapers, but she has begun to signal to me whenever she needs to use the restroom.

Physically, she seems to be gaining balance and motor skills every day. She can now sit up by herself in a straight-back chair, and she can even walk with assistance! I would say that her balance has improved 70 percent in only one short month! At our last checkup, the doctor was surprised by the change he saw in her. And best of all, I know she is happier because she smiles much more often than before.

I am so relieved by the healing that Brain Wave Vibration has brought to my daughter. Before, I sometimes felt so hopeless, wondering if I would be changing diapers for the rest of my life. Now, I have a source of hope for myself and for my daughter. And I have found a wonderful way to connect with my daughter, which, as any parent of an autistic child knows, is a great, great gift.

—Anna Contreras, Henderson, NV

When we face physical difficulties, it is easy to fall into depression. Imagine how difficult it would be to have illness after illness throughout childhood and adulthood, and then end up as a paraplegic. That is the case for the following man, yet he has kept positive through it all. And best of all, he wants to share his healing with others in need.

My problems started as soon as I was born. I was born with an undescended testicle, which was removed at age five. Later I developed cancer in the remaining testicle. In the process of treatment, I contracted hepatitis C through a contaminated blood transfusion. The hepatitis eventually damaged my liver, which required surgery to correct. During the surgery, my spinal cord was damaged, resulting in paralysis from the chest down. On top of that, over the years I have survived four strokes, diabetes, hypertension, and immune system failure.

I liked the idea of Brain Wave Vibration because I figured that was the one thing in my body that was still working! And, after all, the brain controls it all. During Brain Wave Vibration, I was amazed that my shoulders, chest, stomach, and hips all moved together in sync. This should be impossible due to my injury, and yet it happens.

During Brain Wave Vibration, I forget the rest of the world, and I concentrate on what is happening in my body. My doctor told me I would never again feel anything from the rib cage down, yet I am doing just that. I believe that this is happening because of Brain Wave Vibration, which is putting me more in tune with what my brain is saying.

This practice is giving me great hope that eventually I can do more with the muscles in my body. After only one and a half months, I have normalized my liver function, glucose level, and blood pressure. In addition, I have lost fourteen pounds.

My goal is to become a paraplegic yoga master who teaches Brain Wave Vibration. I want to reach out to paraplegics and quadriplegics at the local VA hospital. Whatever their condition, their brain is still there and still working. With this sort of practice, they can keep it working and help it work better. They can alleviate their condition and become more productive so they don't feel as though they are worthless. They can realize they are somebody. They will think, "Hey! If Charles is doing it, we can do it!"

—*Charles Salley, Tacoma, WA*

appendix II

Scientific Investigation
of Brain Wave Vibration and the Brain Education Method

In recent years, scientists have become increasingly interested in studying the effectiveness of Brain Wave Vibration and the Brain Education method. This sort of study is still in its infancy, and it will take many more years of study to conclusively confirm the efficacy of these methods through the scientific method. The most convincing confirmation of their effectiveness remains the stories and experiences of those who have experienced Brain Wave Vibration and Brain Education directly and personally (see page 205-243). As the three studies below indicate, however, early indications suggest that these methods are indeed effective and deserving of further study.

1. Brain Wave Vibration and Stress Hormones

Japanese researcher Arita Hideo of the Medical School of Toho University studied the effects of Brain Wave Vibration on stress hormones. He presented his findings at the Second International Brain Education and Brain Wave Vibration Seminar on November 9, 2008, at the Osaka International Conference Room in Japan.

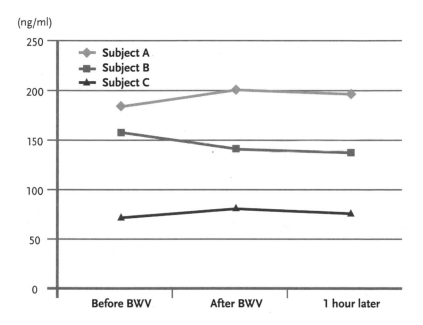

[Serotonin Levels before and after Brain Wave Vibration (BWV)]

Serotonin is a chemical messenger in the brain. The professor's experiment showed a direct correlation between Brain Wave Vibration (BWV) and increased serotonin activity. Generally, the more serotonin secreted, the happier, more attentive, and more peaceful a person becomes. In fact, in people with depression, serotonin levels are lower than normal.

In his experiment, Prof. Arita observed three experienced Brain Wave Vibration practitioners training on three different occasions. All three followed a thirty-minute routine which included warm-up exercises, fifteen minutes of Brain Wave Vibration, and a short meditation activity. After the session, two of the three showed increase in serotonin production.

For one participant, the serotonin level increased from 186 ng/ml (nanograms per milliliter) to 210 ng/ml. Even more impressive, the serotonin level remained consistent over time, measuring 200 ng/ml one hour after the training. Alpha brain waves also increased after Brain Wave Vibration training for all three participants, suggesting a peaceful, meditative state. These other benefits were also noted:

- Increase in brain blood flow, especially in the prefrontal cortex, which is responsible for high-level tasks such as decision making, creativity, social interactions, and the power of self-restraint.
- Reduction in tension, uneasiness, and fatigue.
- Improved brain vitality to the highest level that had been measured in other experiments on various mind–body methods with a similar purpose.
- Alteration of serotonin nerve pathways, suggesting long-term improvements in brain function.

2. Brain Wave Vibration and Indicators of Mental Health

Komiya Noburu, Ph.D., of Osaka University's Department of Human Sciences, also presented his research on psychological benefits of Brain Wave Vibration at the Second International Brain Education and Brain Wave Vibration Seminar on November 9, 2008. His study consisted of a self-reported survey of seventy new Dahn Yoga members in Japan who joined in January 2008. The Dahn Yoga program in Japan focuses mainly on Brain Wave Vibration practice, but also includes light stretching and energy training. The survey measured eight psychological elements and found positive improvements in each over the first six months of practice. Noburu found that the practitioners improved in all seven areas surveyed.

Survey questions, given before, during, and after the six months of training, measured the following:

- Self-respect
- Social Anxiety
- Perfectionism
- Life Satisfaction
- Positive Thinking
- Loneliness
- Sense of Well-being

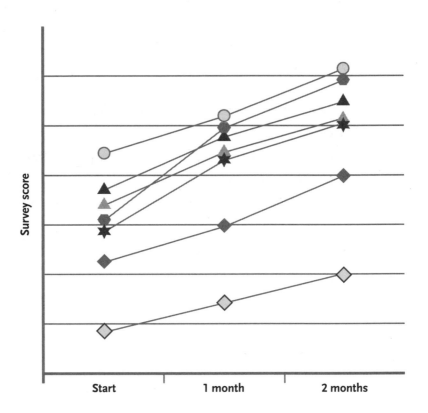

Survey score

Start   1 month   2 months

- Desire to lead a better life
- Sense of well-being
- Life satisfaction
- Self-respect
- Loneliness
- Social anxiety
- Perfectionism

[Brain Wave Vibration and Mental Health]

3. Dahn Yoga Quality of Life Survey

In a study conducted at Whyle Medical College of Cornell University, Dr. Sung Lee studied the outcomes for practitioners who had taken the Dahn Yoga regular class, a component of Brain Education, for three months. The participants were surveyed in eight areas related to quality of life, ranging from general health to social and mental well-being. In other words, these people improved their health, happiness and peace.

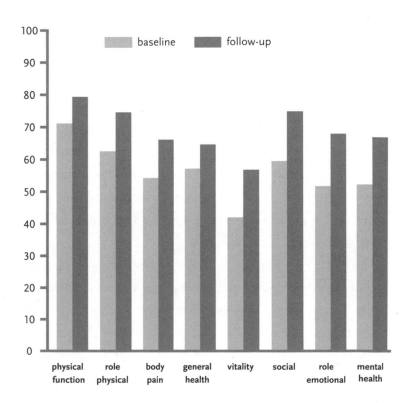

appendix III

HSP Self-Assessment

Examine Your State of Health, Happiness, and Peace

The World Health Organization defines health as "a state of complete physical, mental and social well-being and not merely the absence of disease or infirmity." To achieve a true state of health, the body, mind, and spirit must all work together harmoniously. If a muscular and athletic body is used to perpetrate violence, or if a brilliant mind is used to hurt others through deception, this reflects an unhealthy state.

Although most people desire a state of complete health, the standards by which individual well-being can be measured remain unclear. The HSP (Health, Smile, and Peace) Self-Assessment examines the current state of the three main components of genuine well-being—health, happiness, and peace. The results are then displayed in a diagram that graphically represents your overall state of health.

The HSP Triangle (page 253) is a representation of the well-being of your brain. This is important to consider, since your brain makes all the choices that determine your quality of life. However, it is not a scientific or medical analysis of your brain, and the results are intended only for personal self-reflection.

HSP QUIZZES

Please examine the thoughts, actions, feelings, and attitudes described below and rate each statement, indicating how strongly you agree or disagree with the statement. Rate each statement on a scale of one to five, with one (1) indicating strong disagreement and five (5) indicating strong agreement. After taking all three quizzes, add up all the ratings for each quiz, record them as directed on page 252, and plot the scores on your HSP Triangle on page 253.

Strongly disagree ◄·················► Strongly agree

1	2	3	4	5

Health (H) Quiz

H-1.   I am usually able to breathe naturally and comfortably.

1	2	3	4	5

H-2.   I have plenty of energy throughout the day.

1	2	3	4	5

H-3.   My body usually feels light.

1	2	3	4	5

H-4.   I usually have no trouble moving my neck.

1	2	3	4	5

H-5.   I usually have no trouble moving my wrists and ankles.

1	2	3	4	5

H-6.   I can walk all day without feeling tired.

1	2	3	4	5

H-7.   My arms and legs usually feel strong.

1	2	3	4	5

H-8.   I rarely have headaches.

1	2	3	4	5

H-9.   My mouth usually produces plenty of saliva.

1	2	3	4	5

H-10.   I take time to enjoy my hobbies.

1	2	3	4	5

H-11.   I consume a balanced diet.

1	2	3	4	5

H-12.   I exercise regularly to improve my health.

1	2	3	4	5

H-13.   I sleep deeply and well all night.

1	2	3	4	5

H-14.   I have good digestion.

1	2	3	4	5

Happiness (S) Quiz

S-1.   I always feel good.

1	2	3	4	5

S-2.   I feel I am a happy person.

1	2	3	4	5

S-3.   I have good relationships with my family, coworkers, and other people around me.

1	2	3	4	5

S-4.   I am an optimistic person.

1	2	3	4	5

S-5.   Even if I feel sad about some event in my life, I live with a positive, proactive attitude.

1	2	3	4	5

S-6.   I am very satisfied with my personal, family, and social conditions.

1	2	3	4	5

S-7.   I am grateful for my life as it is now.

1	2	3	4	5

S-8.   I am proud to be who I am.

1	2	3	4	5

Peace (P) Quiz

P-1.   I follow my conscience in all situations.

1	2	3	4	5

P-2.   I am certain that my life is meaningful and purposeful.

1	2	3	4	5

P-3.   I accept difficulties in my life as contributing to my growth.

1	2	3	4	5

P-4.   I am using my talents and abilities in a way that is fulfilling.

1	2	3	4	5

P-5.   I believe that my activities benefit humanity.

1	2	3	4	5

CALCULATING HSP SCORES

Health (H) Quiz (14 items)
Total the points for questions H1–H14. The maximum total is 70 points. ┄┄⟩ Your Health Score: _____ points

Happiness (S) Quiz (8 items)
Total the points for questions S1–S8. The maximum total is 40 points. ┄┄⟩ Your Happiness Score: _____points

Peace (P) Quiz (5 items)
Total the points for questions P1–P5. The maximum total is 25 points. ┄┄⟩ Your Peace Score: _____points

HSP TRIANGLE

After determining your scores in each category, plot the numbers on the following graph, marking your results for each of the three quizzes of health, happiness, and peace. Then connect the points to create a triangle. The larger the triangle and the more equilateral, the greater your overall level of health.

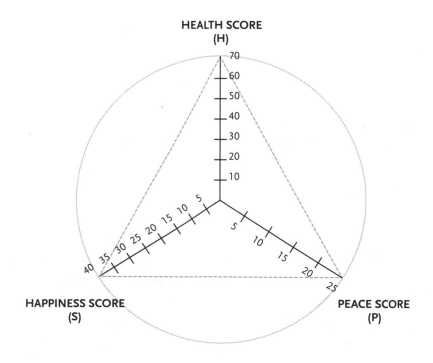

HOW TO IMPROVE YOUR HSP

Improve Your Health

- Breathe comfortably, quietly feeling your breath going in and out. When you are breathing regularly, close your eyes and breathe in and out deeply, and continue this deep breathing for five minutes.
- Practice exercises that gently increase flexibility in your joints and muscles.
- Do exercises that develop strength in your muscles.
- Walk energetically for at least 30 minutes every day.
- Refrain from smoking, consuming excessive amounts of alcohol, and overeating.
- Do not engage in any drug abuse.
- Maintain a schedule for going to bed and waking up.
- Avoid eating for four hours before you go to bed.
- Enhance your natural healing power through Brain Wave Vibration practice.

Accentuate Your Happiness

- Laugh long and loud for no reason. Laughing enhances your brain's production of endorphins and reduces the production of cortisol, a stress hormone.
- Offer genuine compliments and praise to those around you.
- Have gratitude in your heart and express it to others.
- Do not delay any apologies and make them clear.
- Ask for help when you need it.

- Engage in a hobby that you like.
- Know what you truly want in your life.
- Set an important goal for your life.
- Make positive choices.
- Be proactive in your relationships with others.
- Become successful in achieving your goals, however small, to develop self-confidence.
- Realize that you are the master of your brain, and thus master of your life.
- Develop the ability to control your emotions through Brain Wave Vibration.

Increase Your Peace Index

- Realize that all things are connected; awaken to the oneness of all things.
- Know that the belief that your choices change the world is based not on expectation, but on principle.
- Help others in any way you can.
- Take an interest in the problems of society and participate in collaborative efforts to solve them.
- Know what environmental problems the Earth faces, and start by changing your habits regarding your own lifestyle, such as keeping your thermostat at a lower temperature in the winter, using your car less, or recycling more items.
- Awaken your creative power through Brain Wave Vibration.

The Five Steps of
Brain Education System Training

Brain Education System Training (BEST) is designed to maximize your brain potential so you can live a healthy, happy, and peaceful life. The method is divided into five steps, each one building on the achievements of the last. Generally, the steps are practiced in order as you progress, but they will require continuous practice, and many of the BEST programs use various steps simultaneously. Thus, they do not necessarily need to be completed in order. Brain Wave Vibration, when practiced consistently, can enhance all five stages.

Brain Sensitizing

In this first step, you become aware of your brain and its importance in your life. Much of the work is done on the physical level, since the connection between body and brain is strengthened at this point. Yoga, tai chi, chi gong, and martial arts are examples of mind–body exercises used during this step. As each part of your body is moved, corresponding areas of the brain are also awakened. As a result, balance and coordination improves.

Basic meditation and energy training techniques are used at this stage to help you develop better concentration and heightened awareness. Realizing ki energy as the connection between body and brain, you may begin to challenge habits that negatively affect your body and mind. Breath work is also used to restore energetic balance, release stress, and restoring mental clarity.

Brain Versatilizing

Just as muscles need to be stretched to become more flexible, so does the brain. This step exercises neuroplasticity, the brain's ability to adjust to new environments and learn new things. By challenging your brain to master new tasks, you help it gain new connections and greater capacity to develop new patterns of thought and action. The goal of this step is to create an adaptable brain that can learn quickly and overcome negative habits.

This step is likely to have a profound effect on the quality of your life because you will break destructive mental and physical patterns of behavior while creating new, life-affirming habits. Bad habits can be difficult to break because they become, to some degree, hardwired into the brain through repetition, which solidifies neural connections related to the behavior. Fortunately, the brain never loses the ability to restructure itself, and thus new connections can always be created. This includes the ability to change deeply ingrained prejudices and preconceptions for the creation of a better, more satisfying life.

[BRAIN EDUCATION 5 STEPS]

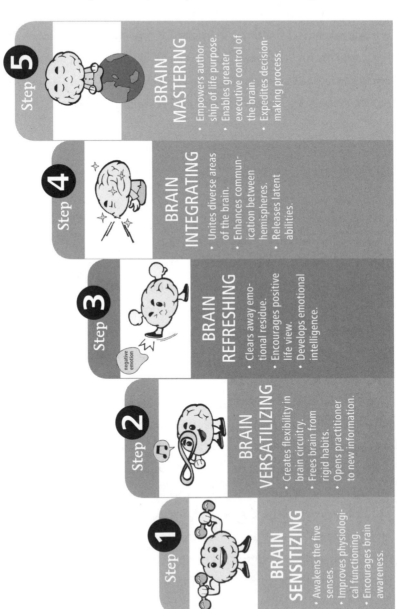

Step 1

BRAIN SENSITIZING

- Awakens the five senses.
- Improves physiological functioning.
- Encourages brain awareness.

Step 2

BRAIN VERSATILIZING

- Creates flexibility in brain circuitry.
- Frees brain from rigid habits.
- Opens practitioner to new information.

Step 3

BRAIN REFRESHING

- Clears away emotional residue.
- Encourages positive life view.
- Develops emotional intelligence.

negative emotion

Step 4

BRAIN INTEGRATING

- Unites diverse areas of the brain.
- Enhances communication between hemispheres.
- Releases latent abilities.

Step 5

BRAIN MASTERING

- Empowers authorship of life purpose.
- Enables greater executive control of the brain.
- Expedites decision-making process.

Brain Refreshing

Throughout life, you experience things have a lasting effect on your brain. These things linger on as a kind of emotional residue that affects your life. These emotions may give rise to preconceptions and negative thought patterns that keep you from reaching your full potential. Brain Refreshing helps release and clear away these burdensome memories to allow healing and renewal.

Through expressing and releasing old emotions rooted in the traumatic experiences of the past, you learn to control the content of your own mind rather than be controlled by the whims of emotional variation. You also learn to use the energy of your mind in a more focused and deliberate way.

Brain Integrating

After you have learned to empty yourself of emotional baggage, you will be ready to expand your awareness and transcend the boundaries of the ego, feeling the oneness of all things. You will be ready to ask yourself fundamental questions about life with complete honesty and sincerity. You will then accept new, positive information into the brain.

Identity is the core information affecting your life, thus it is of primary concern. You can create a new identity based on your newly discovered life purpose. Once you are integrated with this new identity, creative potential becomes practically unlimited.

This stage is called Brain Integrating because all layers of the brain work together. Both hemispheres of the brain communicate better, and disparate parts of the brain work together in full cooperation.

Brain Mastering

Now that you have discovered the life you truly want to live, you are ready to create a lifestyle based on the goals that develop through understanding that purpose. This is essentially a spiritual quest because it requires continuous attention to, and development of, the highest aspects of your character. Brain Mastering cultivates the habit of continuous enlightened living, as opposed to brief, transient moments of enlightenment. During the Brain Mastering phase, you will continue to reapply the four previous steps as you continue to develop your body, mind, and spirit.

Through Brain Mastering, your brain will continue to solidify neural connections that support the creation of a truly happy life. Increasingly, your brain will be able to find creative, workable solutions to the basic problems of life. Also, you will become more naturally decisive, and you will learn to form more peaceful relationships with other people and the world as a whole.

Bibliography

Allen, Colin. "Benefits of Meditation." *Psychology Today,* April 1, 2003.

Alizad, Azra, et al. "Vibrational Characteristics of Bone Fracture and Fracture Repair." *Journal of Biomechanical Engineering* 128.3 (June 2006): 300–309.

Arntz, William, et al. *What the Bleep Do We Know!?* Deerfield Beach, FL: Health Communications, 2005.

Beauregard, Mario, and Denyse O'Leary. *The Spiritual Brain: A Neuroscientist's Case for the Existence of the Soul.* New York: HarperCollins, 2007.

Becker, Robert O., and Gary Selden. *The Body Electric: Electromagnetism and the Foundation of Life.* New York: William Morrow, 1985.

Benson, Herbert. *The Relaxation Response.* New York: William Morrow, 1975.

———. *Timeless Healing: The Power and Biology of Belief.* New York: Scribner, 1996.

Capra, Fritjov. *The Tao of Physics.* Berkeley, CA: Shambhala, 1975.

Cromie, William J. "How Your Brain Listens to Music." *Harvard University Gazette,* November 13, 1997.

Curtis, Diane. "Bridging the Worlds of Neuroscience and Law." *California Bar Journal* (March 2008): 1.

Freeman, W. *How the Brain Makes Up Its Mind.* New York: Columbia University Press, 2000.

Gerber, Richard. *Vibrational Medicine.* 3rd ed. Rochester, VT: Bear and Company, 2001.

Hawkins, David R. *Power vs. Force.* Carlsbad, CA: Hay House, 2002.

Hunt, Valerie V. *Infinite Mind: The Science of Human Vibrations.* Malibu, CA: Malibu Publishing, 1989.

Hutcheon, Bruce, and Yosef Yarom. "Resonance, Oscillation, and the Intrinsic Frequency Preferences of Neurons." *Trends in Neuroscience* 23.5 (May 2000): 216–222.

Kalweit, Holger. *Shamans, Healers, and Medicine Men.* Boston: Shambhala, 2000.

Keeney, Bradford. *Shaking Medicine: The Healing Power of Ecstatic Movement.* Rochester, VT: Destiny, 2007.

Kottler, Jeffrey A., and Jon Carlson with Bradford Keeney. *American Shaman: An Odyssey of Global Healing Traditions.* New York: Routledge, 2004.

Kuby, Lolette. *Faith and the Placebo Effect: An Argument for Self-Healing.* San Rafael, CA: Origin Press, 2004.

Levitin, Daniel J. *This Is Your Brain on Music: The Science of a Human Obsession.* New York: Penguin, 2006.

Lingerman, Hal A. *The Healing Energies of Music.* Wheaton, IL: Theosophical Publishing, 1983.

Lipton, Bruce. *The Biology of Belief: Unleashing the Power of Consciousness, Matter, and Miracles.* Santa Rosa, CA: Elite Books, 2005.

Louv, Richard. *Last Child in the Woods: Saving Our Children from Nature-Deficit Disorder.* Chapel Hill, NC: Algonquin, 2006.

Luerssen, John D. "Beatles Still Reign Supreme among Americans." www.spinner.com, August 14, 2009.

Marion, Matt. "Shake, Rattle, and Stand." *Men's Health,* Jan.–Feb. 2004, 32.

Olof, Johnell, and John Eisman. "Whole Lotta Shakin' Goin' On." *Journal of Bone and Mineral Research* 19.8 (2004): 1205–1207.

Patel, Aniruddh D. *Music, Language, and the Brain.* Oxford University Press, 2008.

Priplatta, Attla, et al. "Vibrating Insoles and Balance Control in Elderly People." *The Lancet* 262 (Oct. 2003): 1123–1124.

Rees, Sven S. "Effects of Whole Body Vibration on Lower-Extremity Muscle Strength and Power in an Older Population." *Physical Therapy* 88:4 (April 2008): 462–470.

Rosenbloom, Stephanie. "What's the Buzz? Sound Therapy." *New York Times,* November 24, 2005.

Sapolsky, Robert M. *Why Zebras Don't Get Ulcers: The Acclaimed Guide to Stress, Stress-Related Diseases, and Coping.* New York: Henry Holt, 1994.

Schwartz, Tony. "Manage Your Energy, Not Your Time." *Harvard Business Review,* October 2007, 63.

Shahidulluh, S., and Pepper, P.G. "Hearing and the Fetus." *International Journal of Prenatal and Perinatal Studies* 4 (1992): 235–240.

Snyder, Solomon H. "Seeking God in the Brain: Efforts to Localize Higher Brain Functions." *New England Journal of Medicine* 358.1 (Jan. 2008): 6.

Stevens, Christine. "Group Drumming Cuts Turnover Rate by 18%." *Occupational Health Management* 14.5 (May 2004): 56.

Thompson, Jeffrey D. "Methods for Stimulation of Brain-Wave Function Using Sound." SelfGrowth.com. http://www.selfgrowth.com/articles/Thompson4.html.

Tomaino, Concetta. "Music Tunes Up the Brain." *Consumer Reports on Health*, February 2009, 6.

Wackermann, Jiri, et al. "Correlations Between Brain Electrical Analysis of Two Spacially Separated Human Subjects." *Neuroscience Letters* 336 (2003):60–64.

Warren, J., et al. "Positive Emotions Preferentially Engage Auditory-Motor 'Mirror' System." *Journal of Neuroscience,* December 12, 2006.

Wayne, Michael. *Quantum Integral Medicine: Towards a New Science of Healing and Human Potential.* Saratoga, NY: iThink Books, 2005.

Winkleman, Michael. "Complementary Therapy for Addiction." *American Journal for Public Health.* 93:4 (April 2003): 647–651.

———. *Shamanism: The Neural Ecology of Consciousness and Healing.* Westport, CT: Bergin and Garvey, 2000.

Index

Resources for Brain Wave Vibration

The following resources will help you get the most out of Brain Wave Vibration training as they expand your awareness of your life and your brain through Brain Education. All books and CDs are available at www.bestlifemedia.com and www.amazon.com.

· BOOKS ·

Principles of Brain Management

A Practical Approach to Making the Most of Your Brain
By Ilchi Lee | $13.95

Drawing from his world-renowned Brain Education method, Ilchi Lee provides readers simple techniques, such as mindful walking, emotional renewal exercises, and basic stress management strategies, to release the brain's creative and cognitive potential. The book offers a clear, down-to-earth presentation of each of the five steps of Brain Education.

In Full Bloom

A Brain Education Guide for Successful Aging
By Ilchi Lee and Jessie Jones, Ph.D. | $18.95

This book explores the brain's remarkable ability to evolve, adapt, and learn at any age. Challenging activities are provided to promote mental quickness and to enhance and support learning throughout life. The book also helps people understand the importance of the brain for emotional patterns and personal identity. In short, this is a book about using the brain's natural abilities to create a happy, productive life in the later years of life.

• AUDIO •

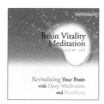

Brain Vitality Meditation CD

By Ilchi Lee | $16.98

This CD contains guidance for all key phases of Brain Education, including Energy Sensitivity training and the five main stages of Brain Education and Power Brain Training. You can follow along through the entire CD or pick a specific track to fit your needs. Discover effective methods for inducing deep relaxation and vitality in the body and brain.

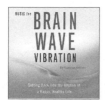

Music for Brain Wave Vibration

By various artists | $17.95

This collection of music is ideally suited to the practice of Brain Wave Vibration. Deeply resonating drum beats will blend naturally with your body's basic rhythms, helping unlock your natural healing abilities. Includes samples of traditional Korean *sa-mul-no-ri*, a style recommended for Brain Wave Vibration practice by its creator Ilchi Lee.

Brain Wave Vibration: Audio Book with a Guided Training Session

By Ilchi Lee | $24.95

The lively spoken-word version of Brain Wave Vibration provides tips for practice and a complete, easy-to-follow training session, as well as profound insights into the nature of human happiness and fulfillment. Also available for download.

Brain Wave Vibration Guided Training CD

Hosted by Melissa Koci | $17.95

Join certified Brain Education instructor Melissa Koci as she guides you through a complete session of Brain Wave Vibration. With her assistance, you will learn to go deeply into the vibration for increased healing and relaxation.

• DVD •

Dahn Yoga Essentials: Featuring Brain Wave Vibration

Hosted by Dawn Quaresima | $19.95

Ilchi Lee developed this dynamic mind–body training system by combining the 5,000-year-old wisdom of Korea with modern understanding of the brain. Join certified instructor Dawn Quaresima as she gently guides you through the healing exercises of Dahn Yoga.

• Internet Resources •

www.brainworld.com

The place to go for everything about the brain. Find brain training tips, up-to-date neuroscience news, and mind-bending games to keep your brain sharp.

www.ilchi.com

Ilchi Lee's official site offers a wealth of information to help you develop your best brain for your best life. Gain insights about the workings of the brain and learn how to make the most of your brain through Brain Education training techniques. Also, you can ask the author questions and gain regular insights through his Ilchi Journal and the Ask Ilchi feature.

www.brainwavevibration.com

An in-depth look at the book *Brain Wave Vibration*, this site offers support for your practice with up-to-date information about Brain Education and related training methods. Visit today and gain a wealth of information about the book, the practice, and the author.

• Individualized Instruction •

Dahn Yoga Centers/ Body+Brain Centers

These centers provide a variety of instruction programs based on Ilchi Lee's Brain Education method, including Brain Wave Vibration. A trained instructor will guide you through the process of setting and achieving goals toward the creation of genuine health and happiness.
www.dahnyoga.com/ www.bodynbrain.com

About the Author

For the past thirty years, Ilchi Lee has dedicated his life to finding ways to develop the potential of the human brain. Brain Education System Training, a collection of mind–body training programs that helps to unlock the brain's true potential, is the primary fruit of his search. The ultimate purpose of brain development, according to Lee, is lasting world peace. He identifies the brain as the seat of human consciousness, and therefore it is through developing the brain that he believes humanity may transcend its current condition.

Currently, Lee serves as the president of the University of Brain Education and the Korea Institute of Brain Science. Lee is the author of more than thirty books, and his work as a pacemaker and educator has been widely recognized, both in his native Korea and in the international community.